RECORDED VERSIONS
GUITAR

AUTHENTIC TRANSCRIPTIONS
WITH NOTES AND TABLATURE

FRANK ZAPPA Over-Nite Sensation

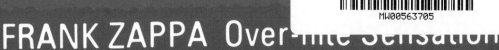

Music & Lyrics by Frank Zappa

Transcriptions by Paul Pappas

ISBN 978-0-634-06110-3

HAL•LEONARD®
CORPORATION
7777 W. BLUEMOUND RD. P.O. BOX 13819 MILWAUKEE, WI 53213

Visit Hal Leonard Online at
www.halleonard.com

Anything Zappanese go to
www.zappa.com

forward

by warren cuccurullo

WHEN music that is not NORMAL is outlawed, your'e gonna thank me for telling you to buy extra copies of this book... you will bury them in a lead box at a secret location...and trust me...they WILL be starting with the Z's.. when i was 16 & i bought my first zappa record (this one) i had committed the entire disc to memory & i would get on the subway & "put it on" in my head & let it play...i would start with zomby woof...this is pre-walkman daze... & every note was there...by the time i got to the montana solo, i couldn't believe the other people on the train weren't hearing it...so, you might wanna do the same...just in case it's all DELETED...

frank zappa wasn't just the guy with the coolest muckin fustache ever, WE all know he was the greatest guitarist/composer of the 20th century...(he always said i was easily amused). i spent most of my time between the age of 16 & 22 trying to convince anyone who liked music that they could LOVE zappa...i saw *this* band in 1973 at Brooklyn College...it was REAL magic...frank on one side of the stage with george behind him, & this girl ruth, who frank would talk to, doing the most amazing things on the other... & the singer's name was napoleon...i was ecstatic...sounds that i only heard before in cartoons, or in scores of films were all there, even munchkins...the guitar playing was unique... melodic & angry...& it fit PERFECTLY with his songs...the riffs he wrote,...heavier & harder than all the zeppelin, deep purple & sabbath stuff that i'd regurgitated for years...overnite was my secret weapon when i was turning people on to frank,.. a fun process indeed... & i could easily support my best guitar player argument with it...
this is one of the dream mothers lineups & arguably the best ever assembled in ANY genre... frank, ian , ruth, george AND the fowlers!!! genius, chemistry, personality, what frank did was simply musical entertainment at it's finest...but, not just for distraction's sake...if you LISTEN to zappa you can learn...not just about music...he kept a lot of kids away from drugs, he made you consult the dictionary now & again, he encouraged going to the library to seek out information for yourself...& he explained everything you needed to know about groupies, absurd fetishes & life on the road...these would prove invaluable to me...what a role model i chose...THIS JUST IN: did you ever entertain the fact that some of YOUR favorite rockstars of this gaLORious era might've been delving deeper into their drug use not just due to *subconscious tension*, but because they might've been trying to figure out what concoction frank was using? maybe they heard about his dad being a chemist...

frank vincent zappa was & will forever be the wizard of odd times...the great imaginer...the greatest organizer of sound events & words in history...& let me tell ya, a hell of a great person & friend...the most giving, honest, sensible, hardworking, & special human being ever created...he had a magical presence, an energy you could feel...he was electric....& i loved him & his music more than anything in my life...more importantly, my life as i know it would not exist without him..quite the Mother....
when i was a kid in the audience with tears of joy streaming down my face, like they are now, or when i was on stage playing with him, the words i most dreaded hearing would come all too often for me..."we'd like to thank you very much for coming to our concert tonight..."
PLEASE COME BACK FOR AN ENCORE....

wc 21 12 07

Camarillo Brillo

By Frank Zappa

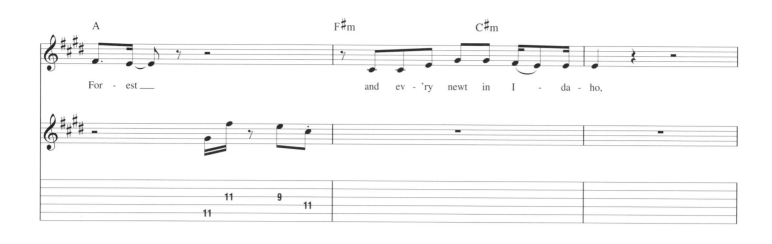

For - est ___ and ev - 'ry newt in I - da - ho,

and ev - 'ry crick-et who had cho - rused ___ by the bush in Buf - fa - lo. ___

Gtr. 3 tacet

___ She said she was ___ a Mag - ic Ma - ma

*Gtr. 4

mf

*Piano arr. for gtr.

and she could throw a mean ___ tar - ot, and car - ried on, _____ with-out a com-

Gtr. 4 tacet

Gtr. 4

Gtr. 3

Gtr. 3
divisi

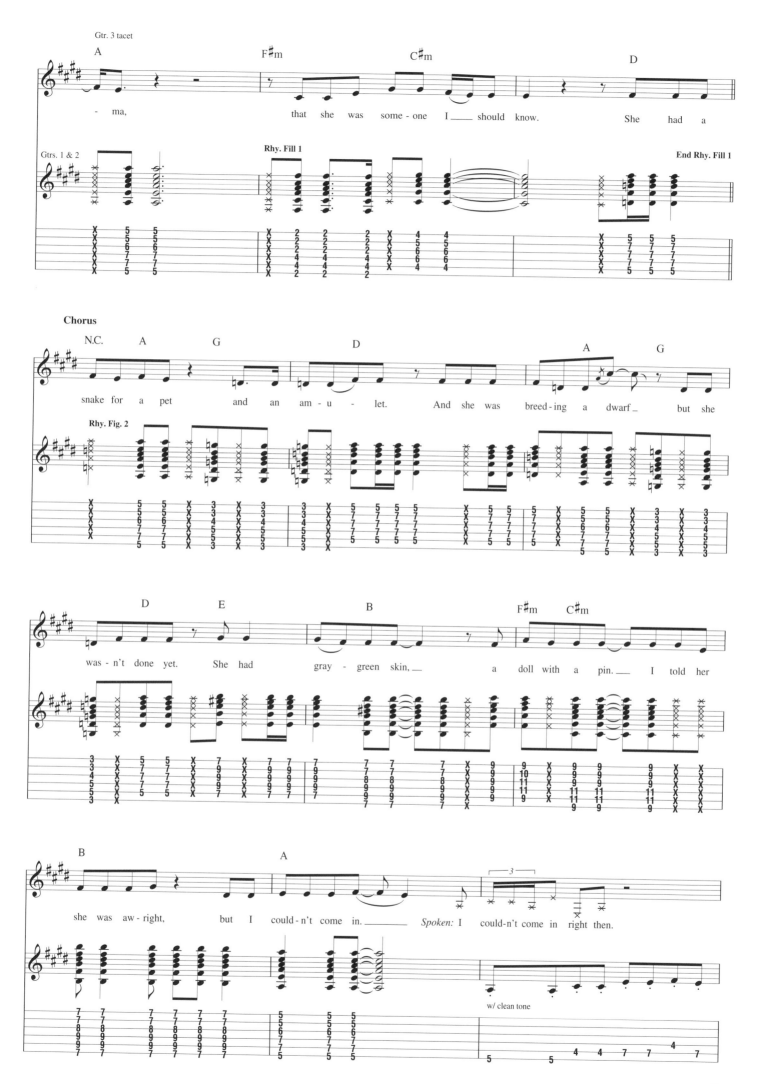

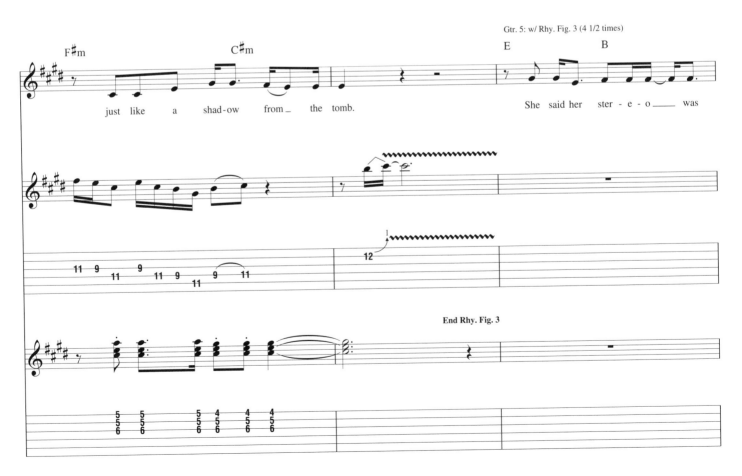

four - way, __ an' I'd just love it in her room. _____

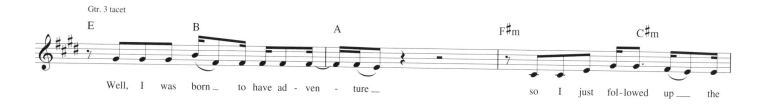

Well, I was born __ to have ad - ven - ture __ so I just fol - lowed up __ the

steps, __ right past her fum - ing in - cense __ stench - er

to where she hung her cas - ta - nets. She stripped a - way __ her ran - cid

ponch - o ___ an' laid out na - ked by ___ the door.

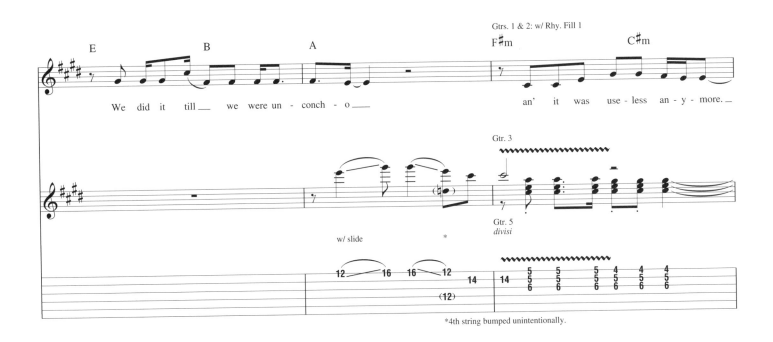

We did it till ___ we were un - conch - o ___ an' it was use - less an - y - more. ___

*4th string bumped unintentionally.

Chorus

She had a snake for a pet and an am - u - let. And she was

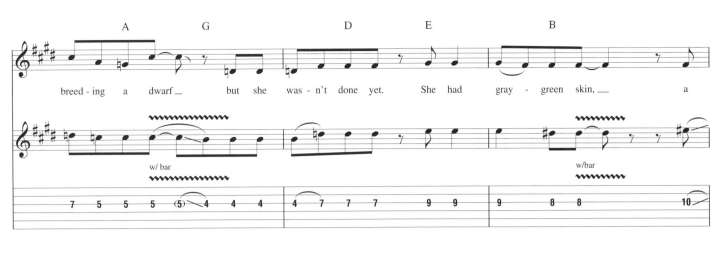

breed-ing a dwarf __ but she was-n't done yet. She had gray - green skin, __ a

doll with a pin. __ I told her she was aw - right, but I could - n't come in. __

Verse

Gtrs. 1 & 2: w/ Rhy. Fig. 1 (6 times)

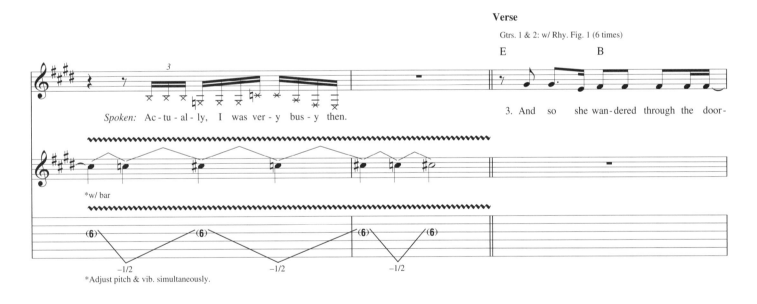

Spoken: Ac - tu - al - ly, I was ver - y bus - y then.

3. And so she wan - dered through the door-

*w/ bar

*Adjust pitch & vib. simultaneously.

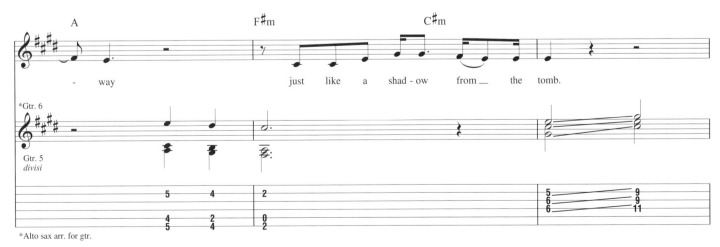

- way   just like a shad - ow from __ the tomb.

*Gtr. 6

Gtr. 5
divisi

Alto sax arr. for gtr.

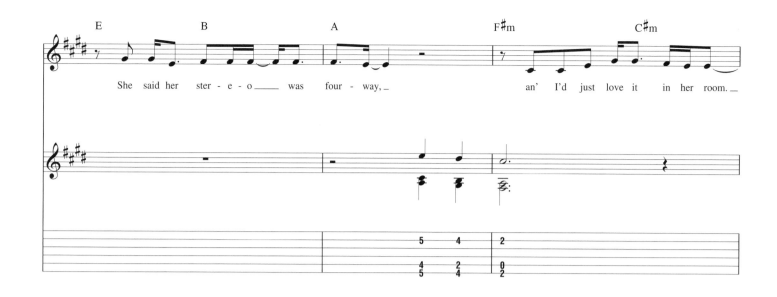

She said her ster - e - o _ was four - way, _ an' I'd just love it in her room. _

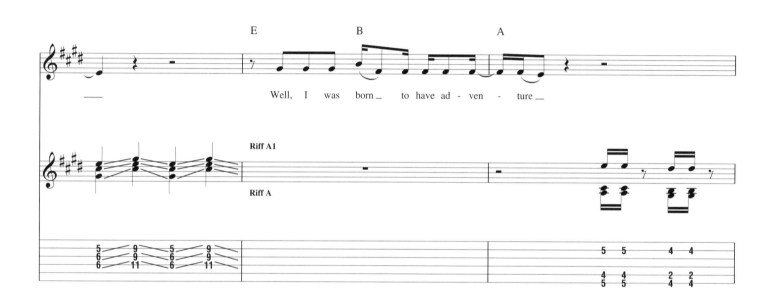

— Well, I was born _ to have ad - ven - ture _

Riff A1

Riff A

so I just fol-lowed up _ the steps, right past her fum-ing in - cense _

*Notes in parentheses are played only when Riffs A & A1 are recalled.

___ stench - er   to where she hung her cas - ta - nets.

Gtr. 3

w/o slide

Gtr. 6

End Riff A1

Gtr. 5

End Riff A

Gtr. 3 tacet
Gtrs. 5 & 6: w/ Riffs A & A1

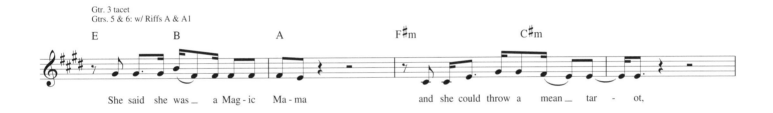

E   B   A   F#m   C#m

She said she was ___ a Mag - ic Ma - ma   and she could throw a   mean ___ tar - ot,

E   B   A   F#m   C#m

and car - ried on, _____ with - out a com - ma,   that she was some - one I ___ should know.

Outro

Gtrs. 1 & 2: w/ Rhy. Fig. 1 (till fade)
Gtrs. 5 & 6: w/ Riffs A & A1 (till fade)

E   B   A   F#m   C#m

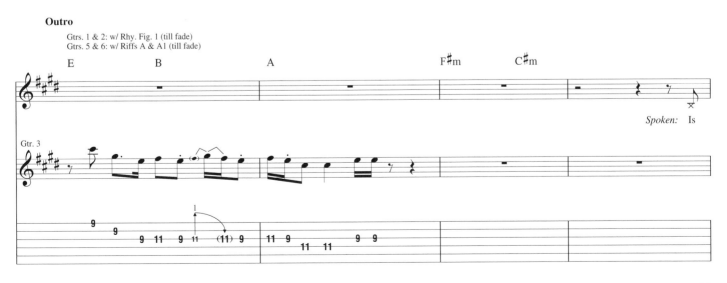

Spoken: Is

Gtr. 3

15

I'm the Slime

By Frank Zappa

Intro
Free time

*Chord symbols reflect overall harmony.

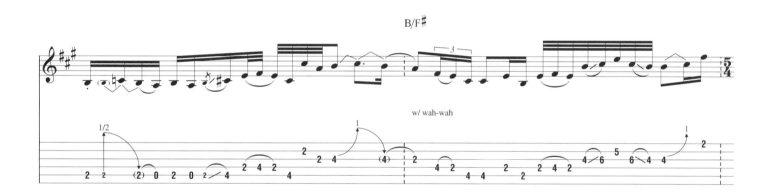

w/ wah-wah

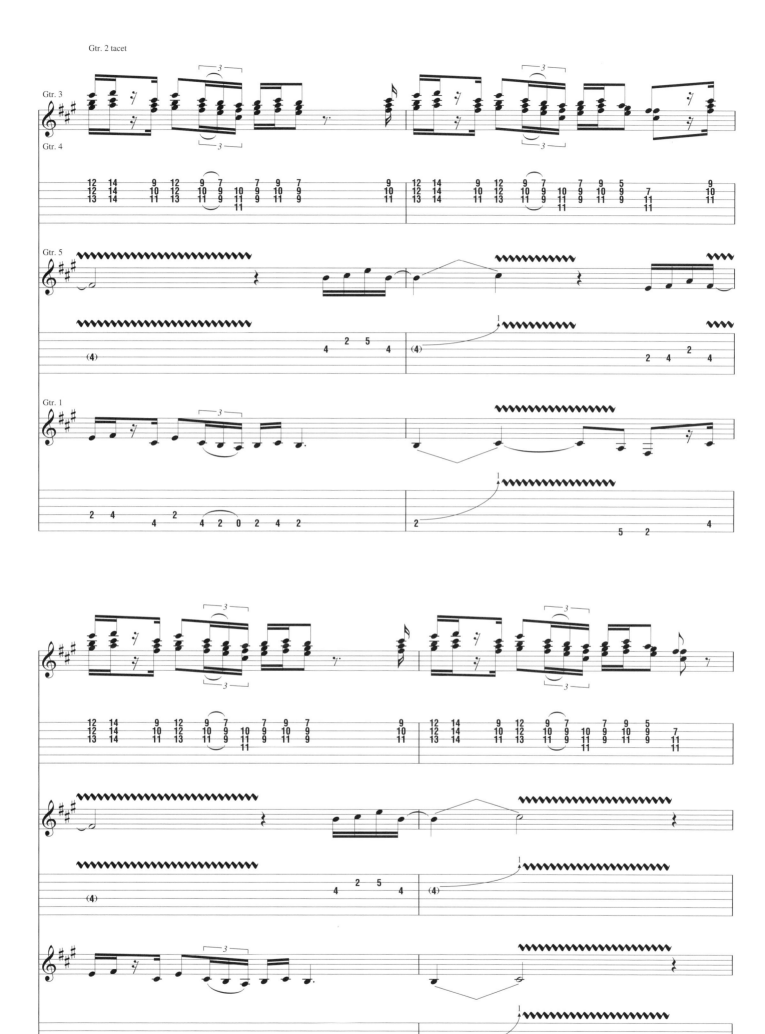

Verse

Gtrs. 1, 3, 4 & 5 tacet

Dm7

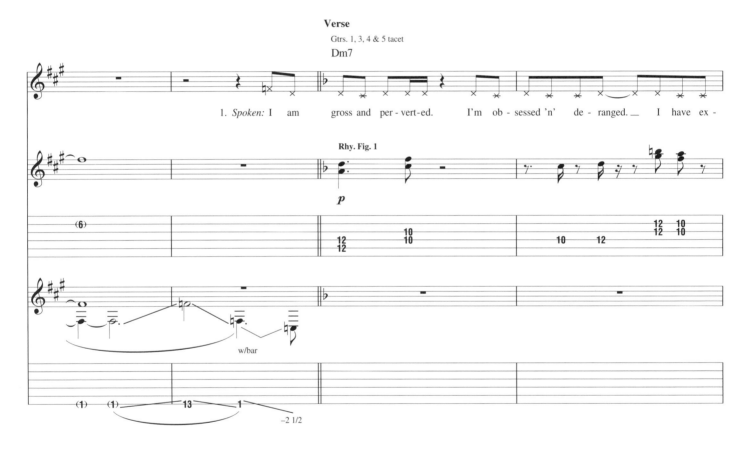

1. *Spoken:* I am gross and per-vert-ed. I'm ob-sessed 'n' de-ranged. ___ I have ex-

Gtr. 6: w/ Rhy. Fig. 1 (2 times, simile)

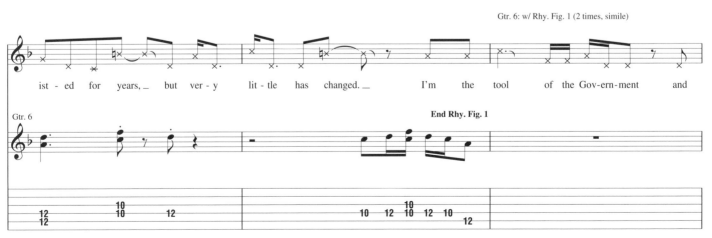

ist-ed for years, ___ but ver-y lit-tle has changed. ___ I'm the tool of the Gov-ern-ment and

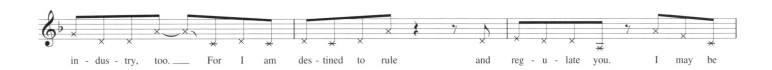

in - dus - try, too.___ For I am des - tined to rule and reg - u - late you. I may be

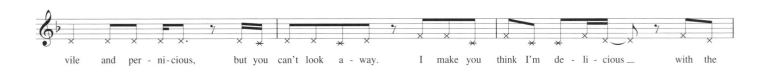

vile and per - ni - cious, but you can't look a - way. I make you think I'm de - li - cious___ with the

stuff that I say. I'm the best you can get. Have you guessed me yet? I'm the

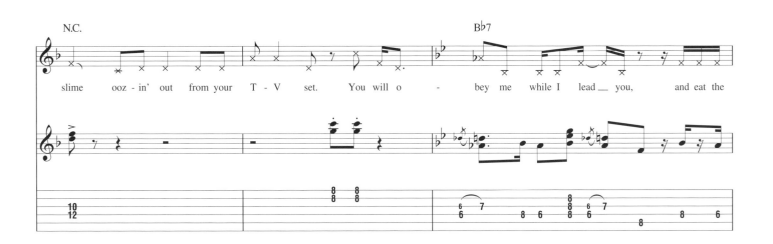

slime ooz - in' out from your T - V set. You will o - bey me while I lead___ you, and eat the

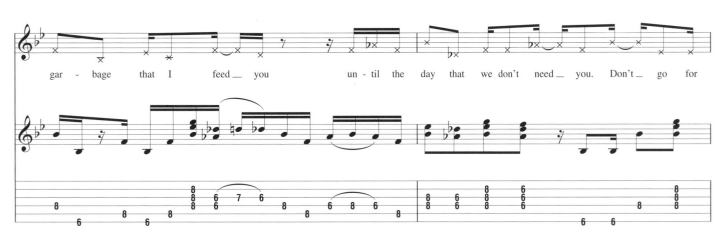

gar - bage that I feed___ you un - til the day that we don't need___ you. Don't___ go for

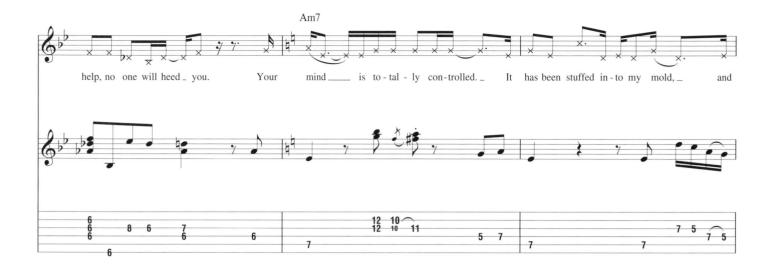

help, no one will heed you. Your mind is to-tal-ly con-trolled. It has been stuffed in-to my mold, and

you will do as you are told un-til the rights to you are sold.

Interlude

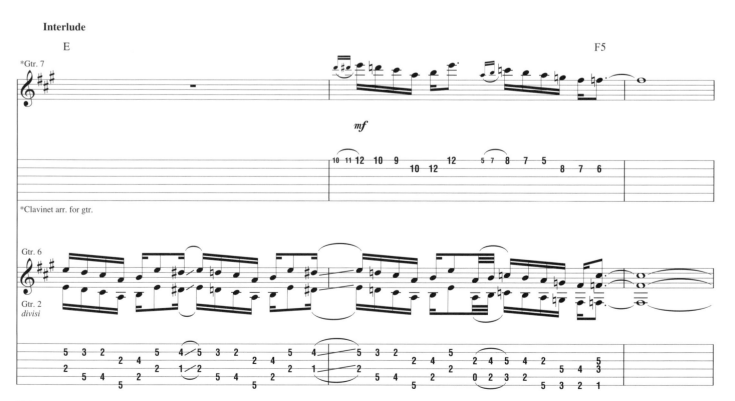

*Gtr. 7

*Clavinet arr. for gtr.

Gtr. 6

Gtr. 2
divisi

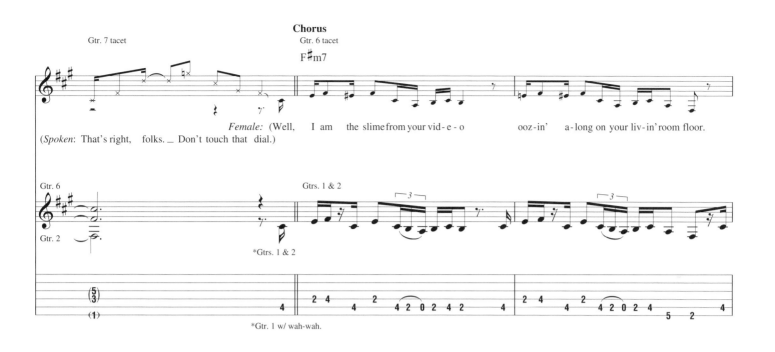

Chorus

Female: (Well, I am the slime from your vid-e-o oozin' a-long on your liv-in' room floor.
(*Spoken:* That's right, folks. __ Don't touch that dial.)

*Gtr. 1 w/ wah-wah.

I am the slime from your vid-e-o. Can't stop the slime, peo-ple look-it me go.

**3rd time, omit last note.

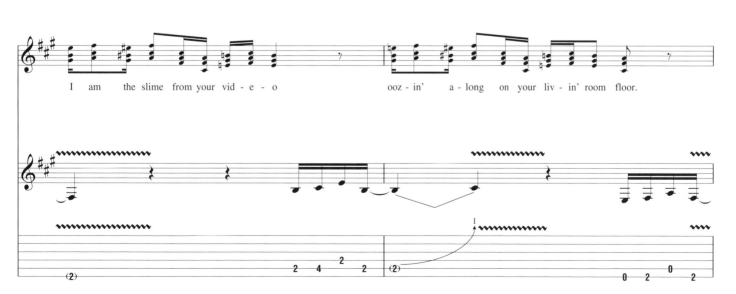

I am the slime from your vid-e-o oozin' a-long on your liv-in' room floor.

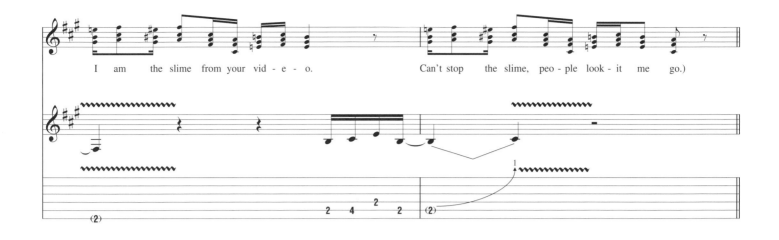

I am   the slime from your vid - e - o.   Can't stop   the slime, peo - ple look - it me   go.)

Outro-Guitar Solo

Gtr. 5 tacet

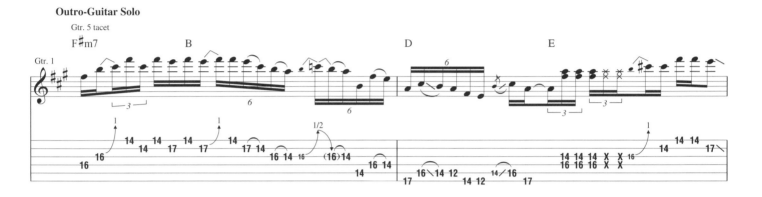

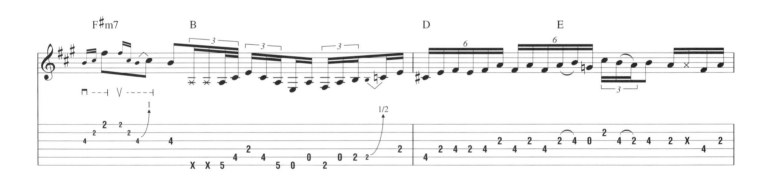

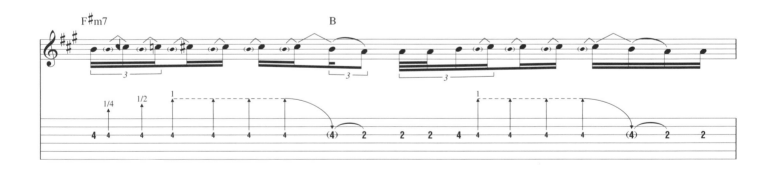

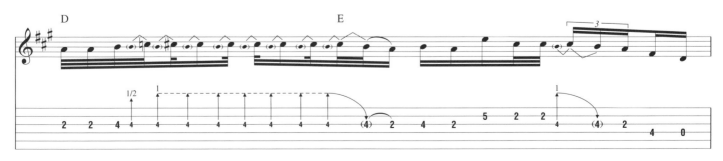

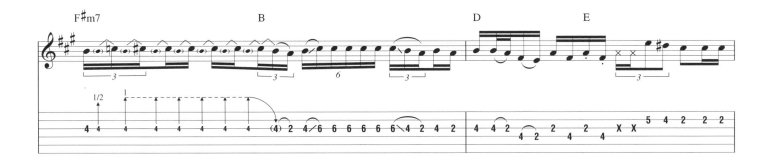

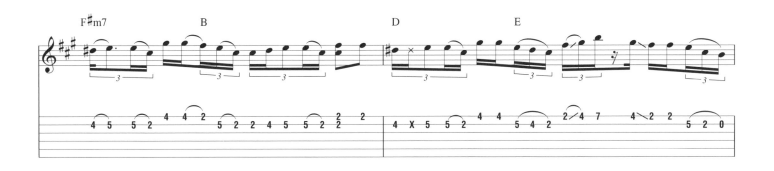

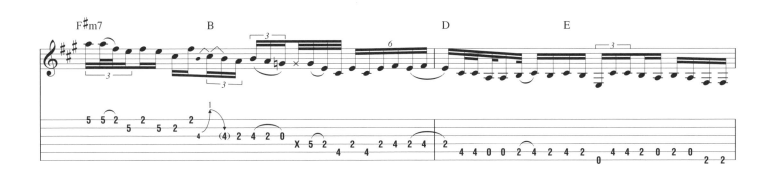

Begin fade

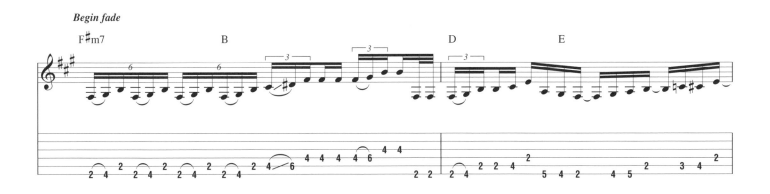

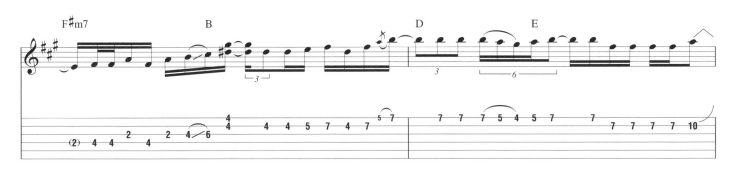

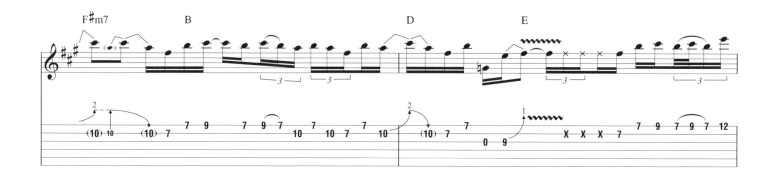

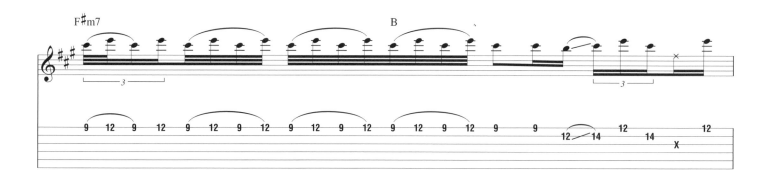

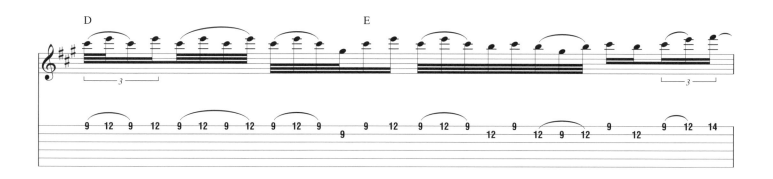

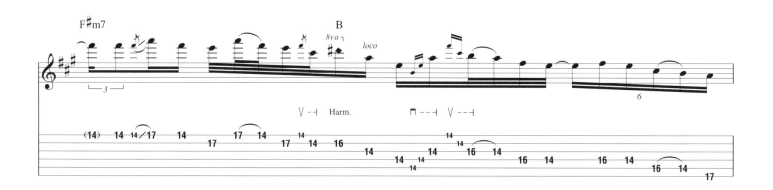

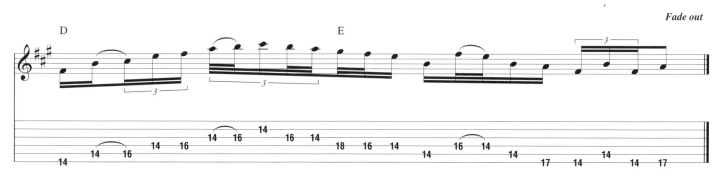

Dirty Love

By Frank Zappa

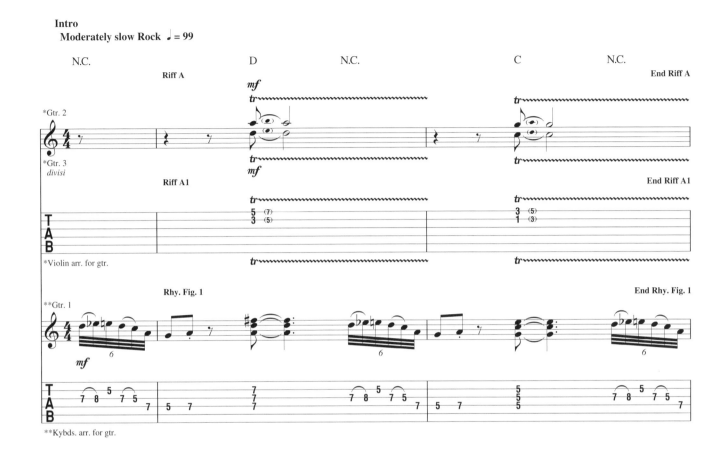

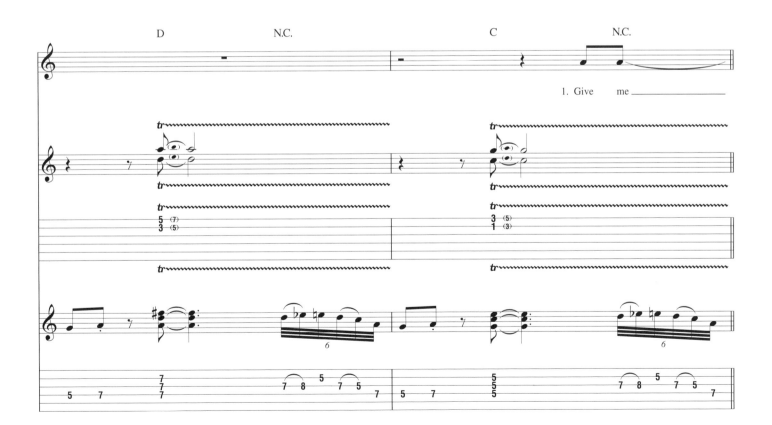

Verse

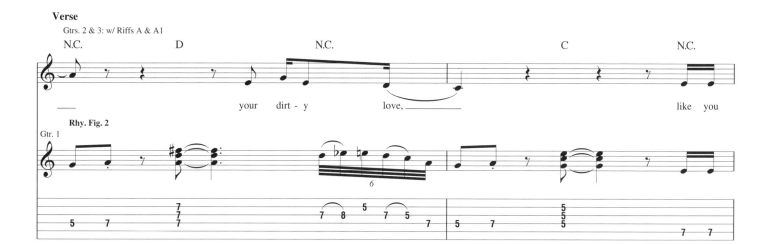

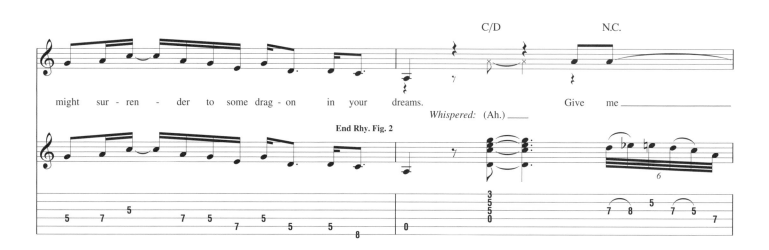

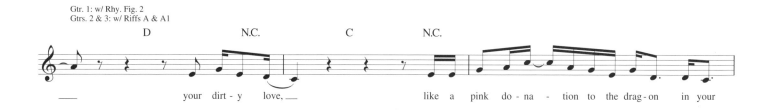

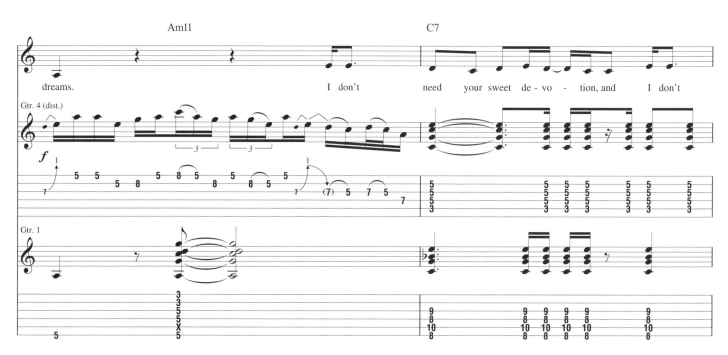

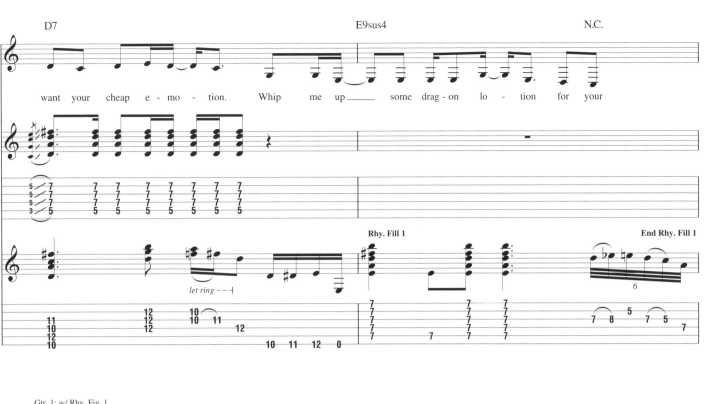

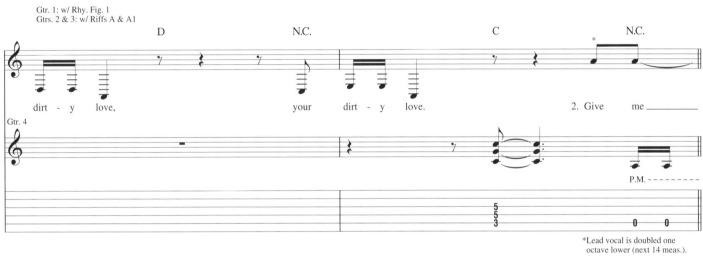

tack - y lit - tle pam - phlet in your dad - dy's bot - tom draw'r. ___ Give me ___

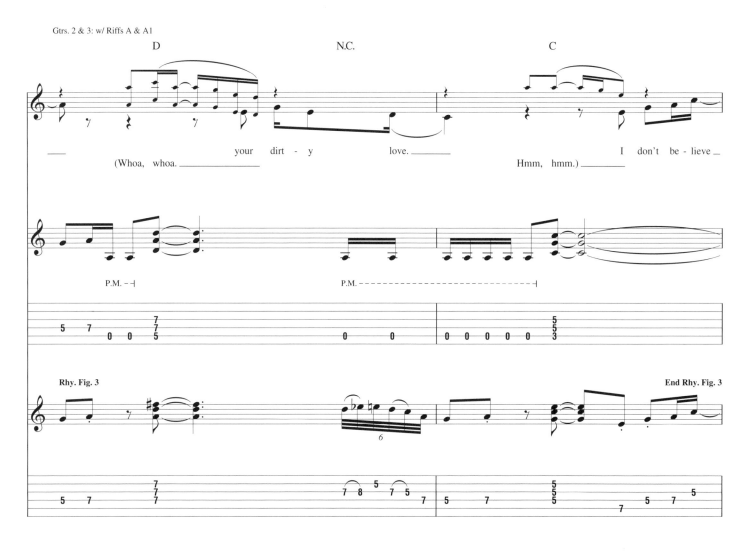

Gtrs. 2 & 3: w/ Riffs A & A1

D   N.C.   C

___   your dirt - y   love. ___   I don't be - lieve ___
(Whoa, whoa. ___   Hmm, hmm.) ___

Rhy. Fig. 3   End Rhy. Fig. 3

30

you nev-er seen his book be-fore.

I don't

need no con-so-la-tion, I don't want your res-er-va-tion. I on-ly

Gtr. 1: w/ Rhy. Fill 1

Gtr. 1: w/ Rhy. Fig. 1
Gtrs. 2 & 3: w/ Riffs A & A1

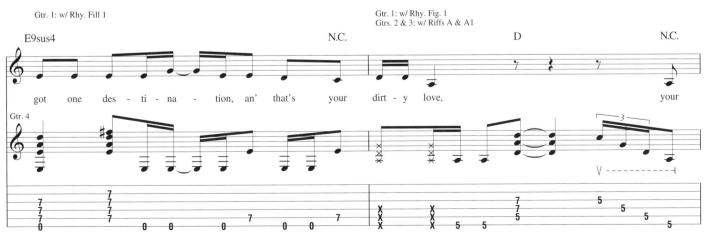

got one des-ti-na-tion, an' that's your dirt-y love,

your

Guitar Solo

Gtr. 1: w/ Rhy. Fig. 1 (3 1/2 times)

dirt - y love.

Gtr. 4

w/ wah-wah

P.H.

*Gtr. 5

mp

*Clavinet arr. for gtr.

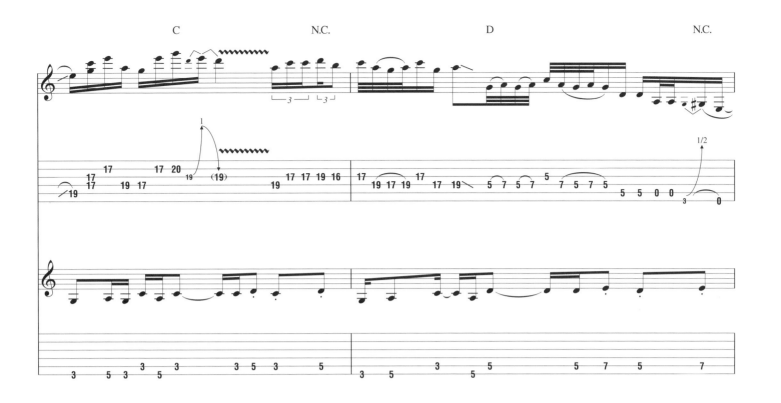

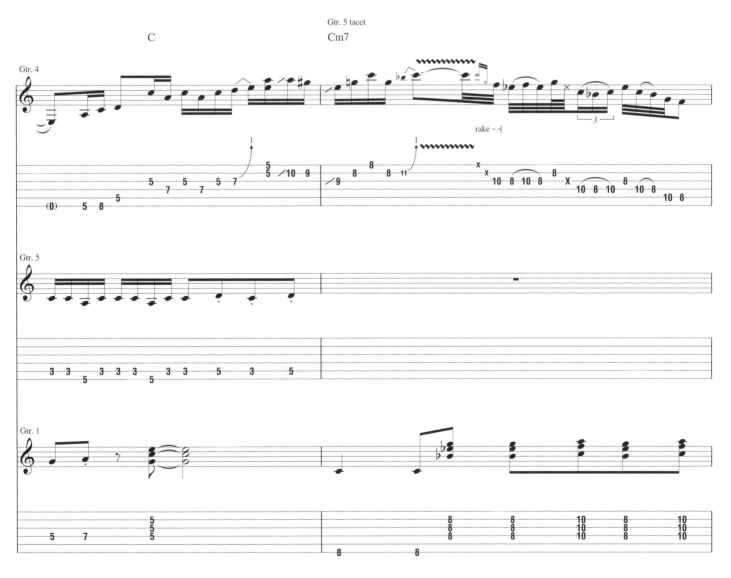

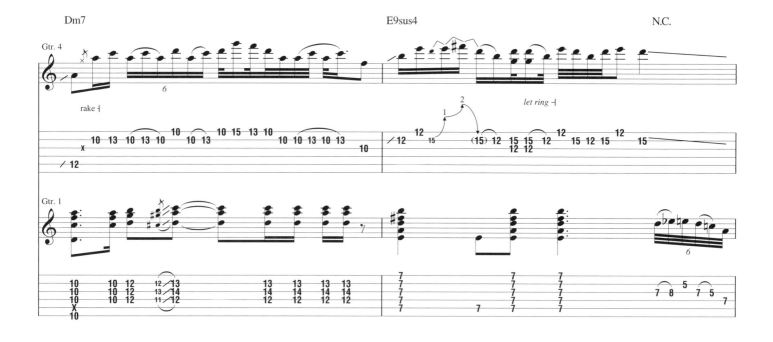

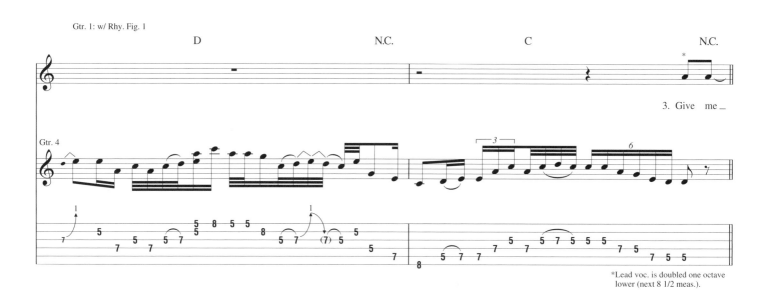

*Lead voc. is doubled one octave
lower (next 8 1/2 meas.).

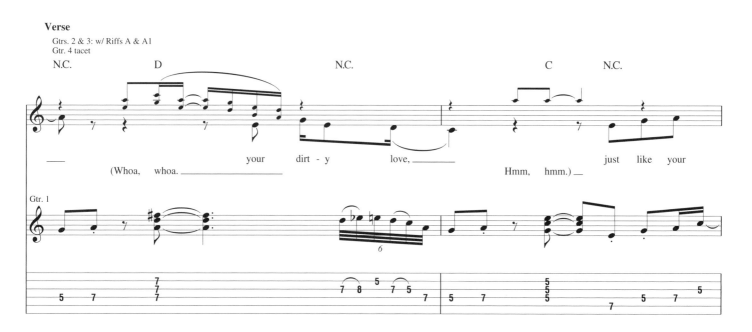

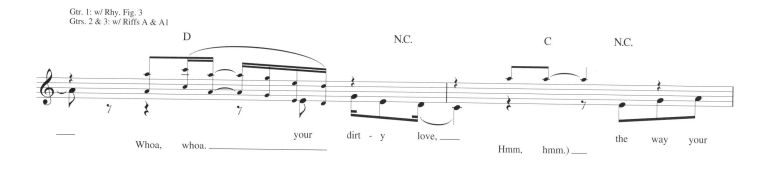

Outro

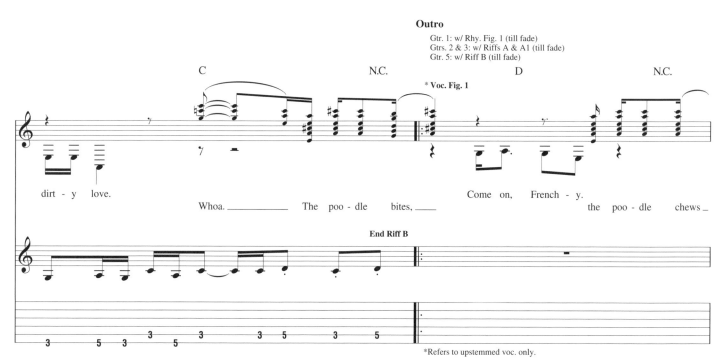

*Refers to upstemmed voc. only.

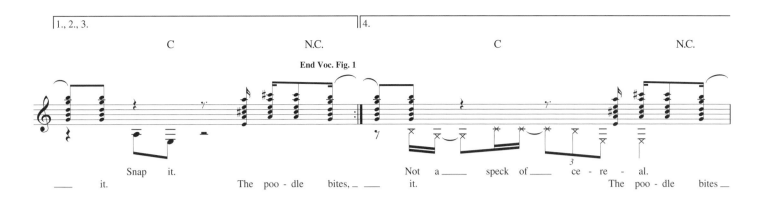

Snap it. The poo-dle bites, ___ it. Not a ___ speck of ___ ce-re-al. The poo-dle bites ___
___ it.

Begin fade

Bkgd. Voc.: w/ Voc. Fig. 1 (till fade)

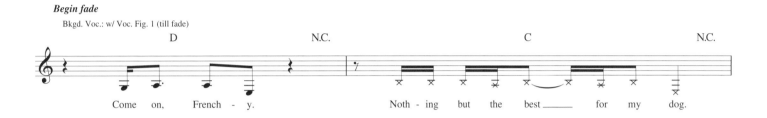

Come on, French - y. Noth-ing but the best ___ for my dog.

Come on, French - y. Come on.

Come on, French - y. Lit - tle paws stick - in' up.

Fade out

Lit - tle curl - y ___ head. Lit - tle curl - y ___ head.

Fifty-Fifty

By Frank Zappa

C7

Intro
Moderate Rock ♩ = 126

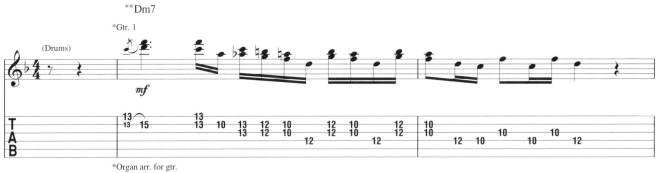

*Organ arr. for gtr.
**Chord symbols reflect overall harmony.

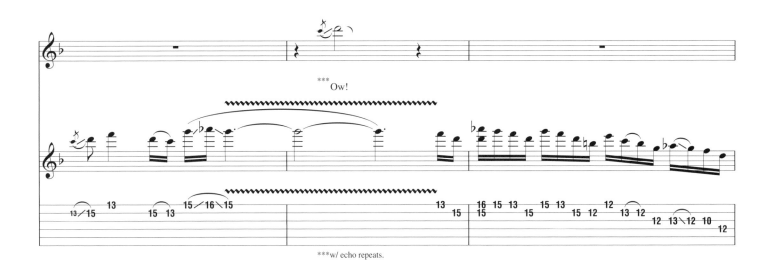

***w/ echo repeats.

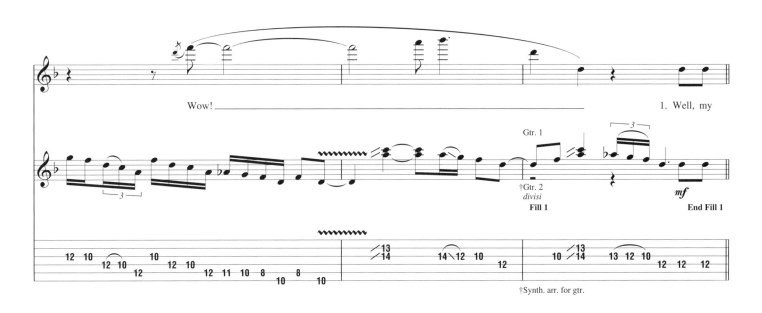

†Synth. arr. for gtr.

Verse

1st time, Gtr. 1 tacet
2nd time, Gtrs. 5 & 7: w/ Riff A
2nd time, Gtr. 6 tacet

dan - druff is loose _____ an' my breath is char - treuse. _____
tak - en your time, _____ I have sung you my song. _____

Riff A

Gtr. 2

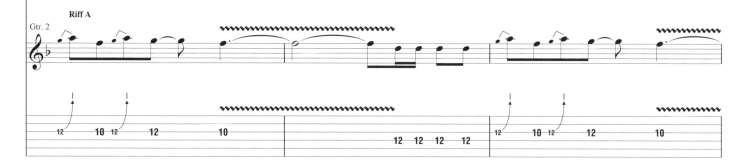

_____ Hoo, hoo. I know I ain't cute _____ an' my
_____ Ain't no great rev - e - la - tion, _____ but it

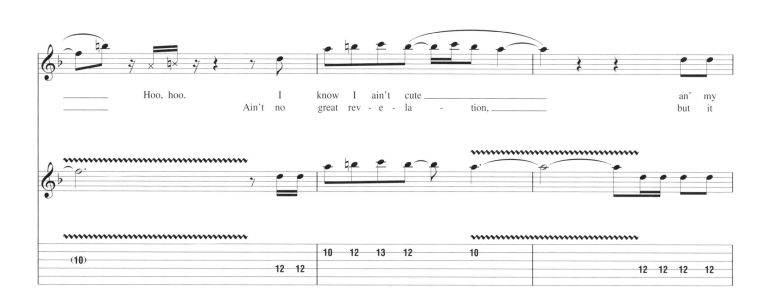

voice is ka - poot. _____ But that's aw - right, peo - ple. _____
was - n't too long. _____ An' that's aw - right, peo - ple. _____

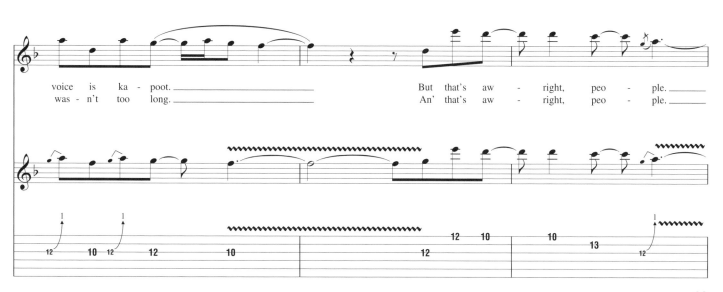

I'm just cra-zy e-nough to sing to you,_____ heh, heh, an-y old way._

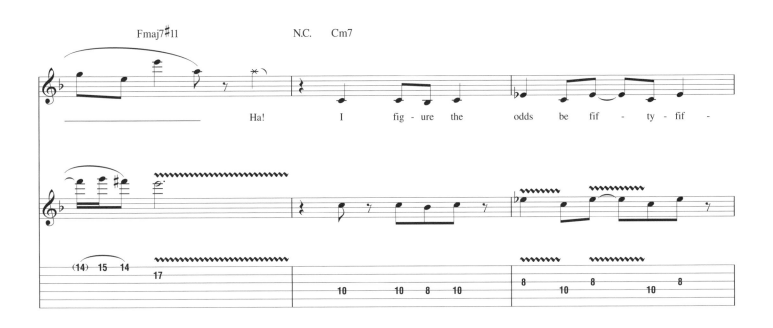

Ha! I fig-ure the odds be fif - ty-fif -

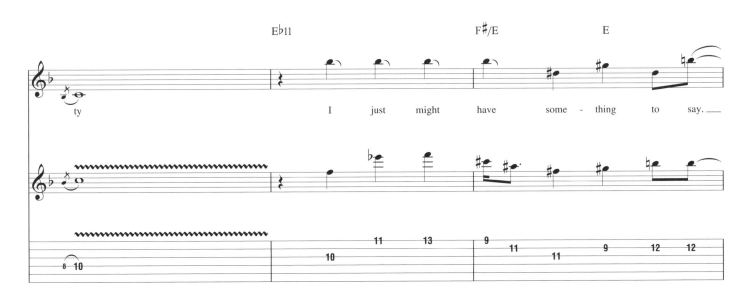

ty I just might have some - thing to say._

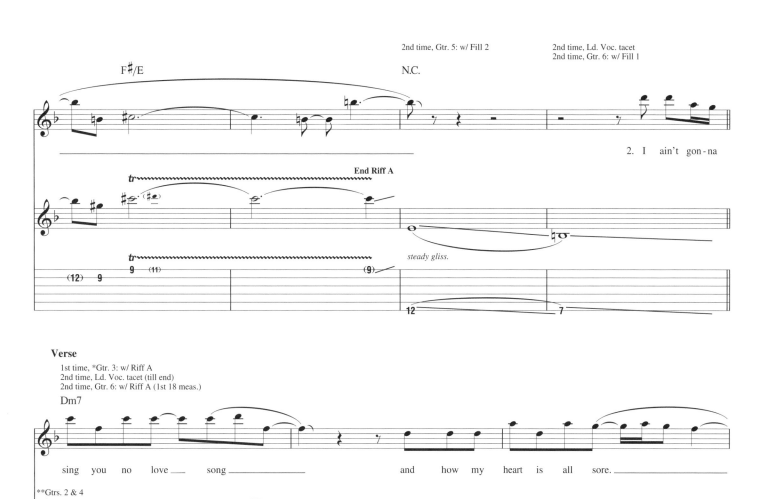

Verse

1st time, *Gtr. 3: w/ Riff A
2nd time, Ld. Voc. tacet (till end)
2nd time, Gtr. 6: w/ Riff A (1st 18 meas.)

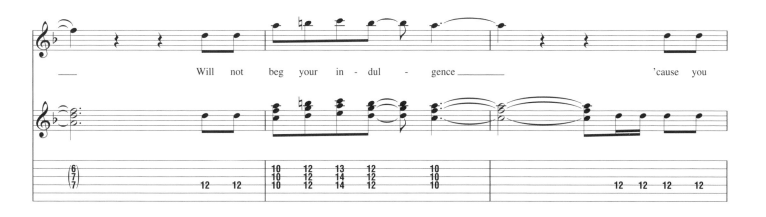

*Trumpet arr. for gtr., played *mf*.
**Gtr. 4 is horns arr. for gtr., played *mf*.

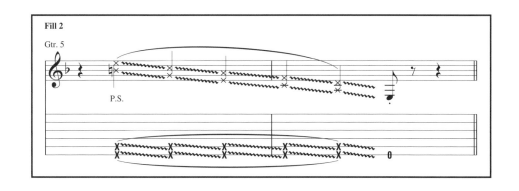

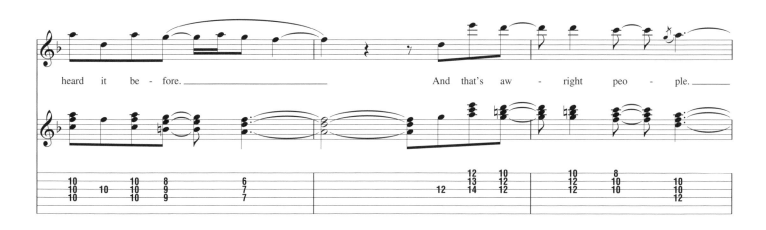

heard it be - fore. _____ And that's aw - right peo - ple. _____

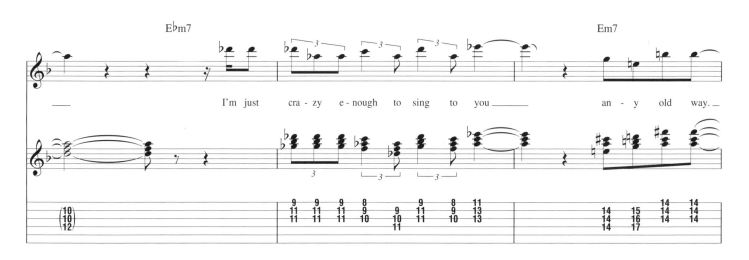

Ebm7

_____ I'm just cra - zy e - nough to sing to you _____ an - y old way. _____

Em7

Fmaj7#11   N.C.   Cm7

_____ Hey! _____ I fig - ure the odds be fif - ty - fif -

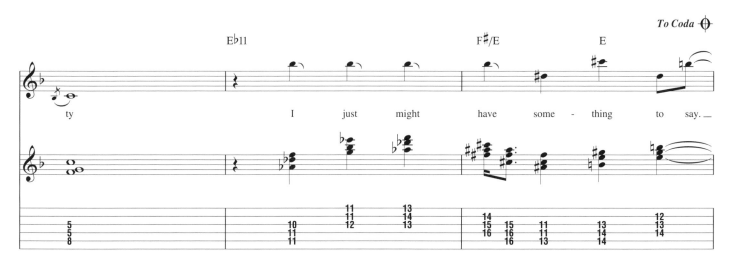

Eb11   F#/E   E

To Coda ⊕

ty   I just might have some - thing to say. _____

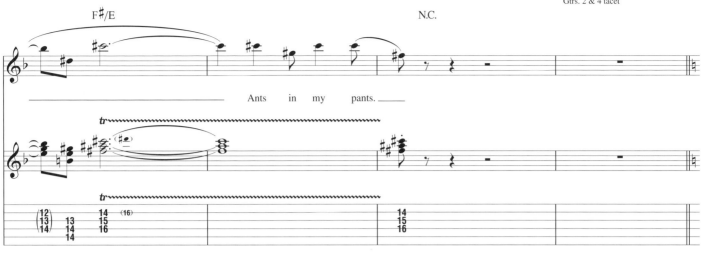

Ants in my pants.

Organic Solo

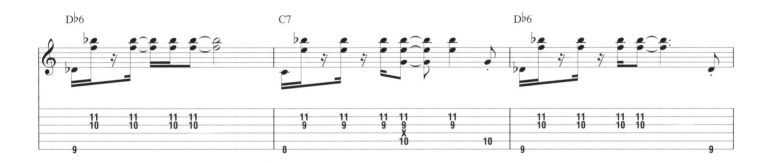

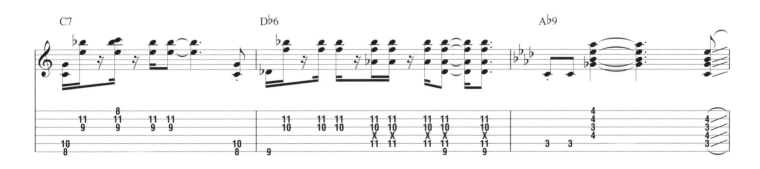

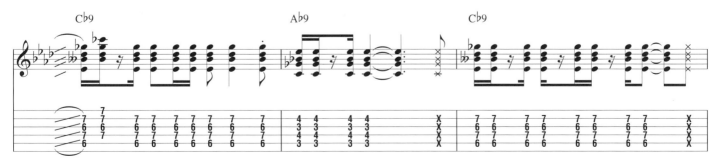

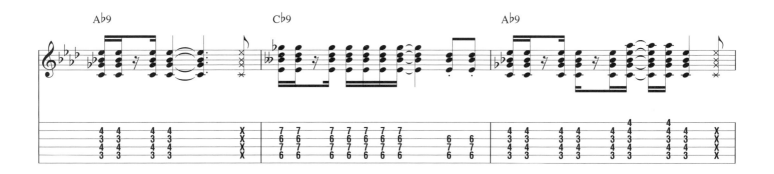

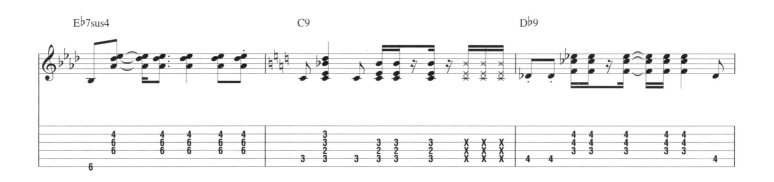

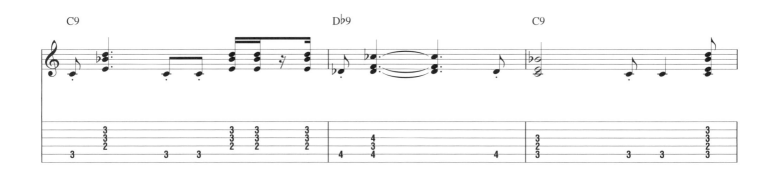

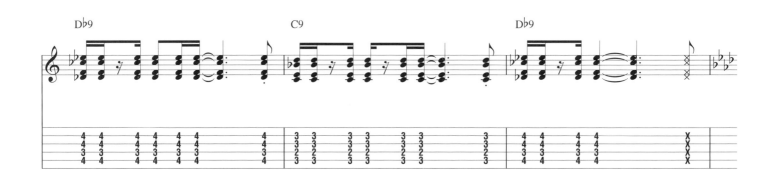

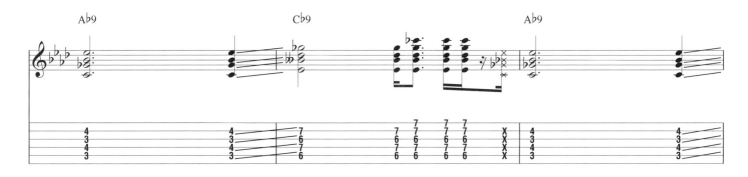

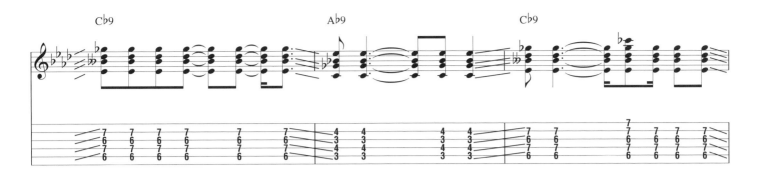

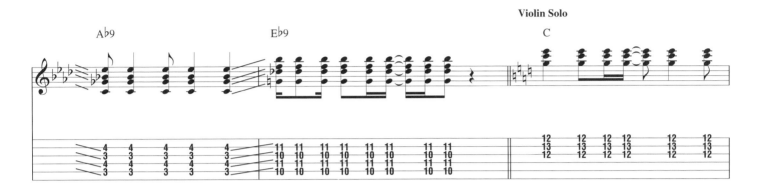

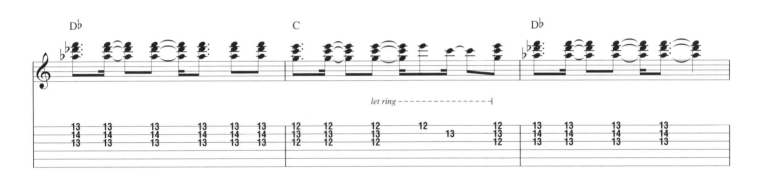

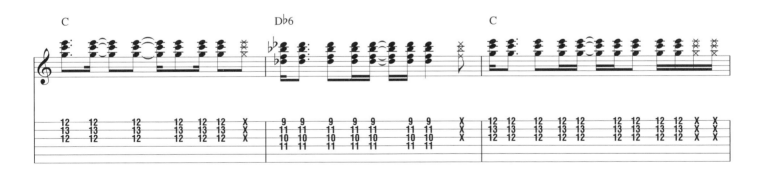

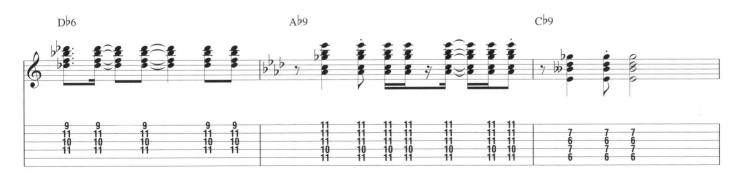

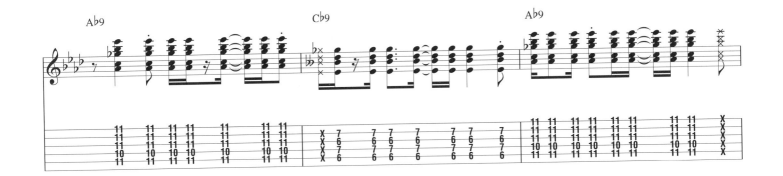

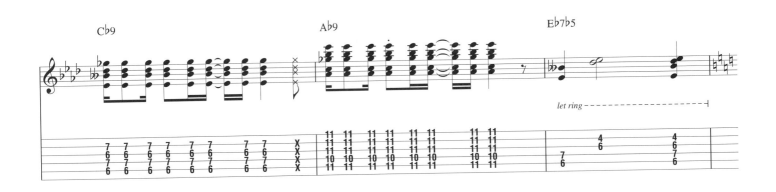

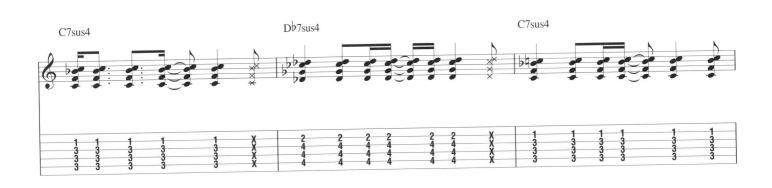

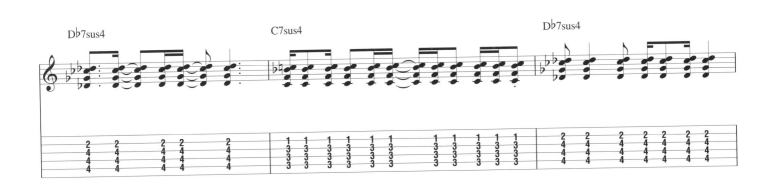

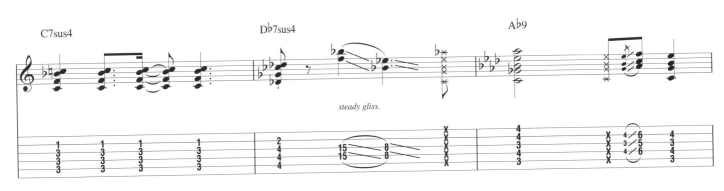

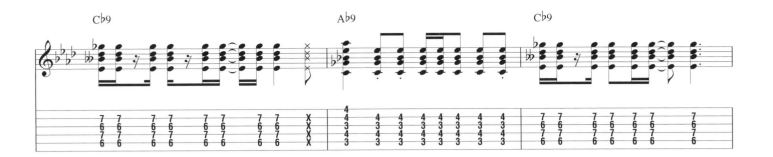

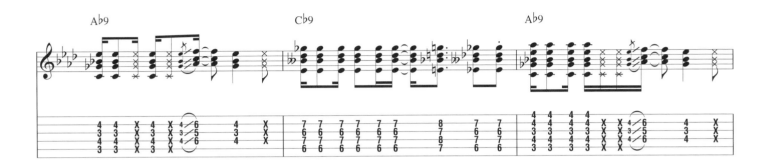

Guitar Solo

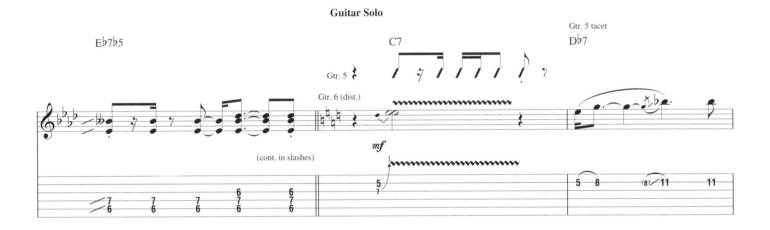

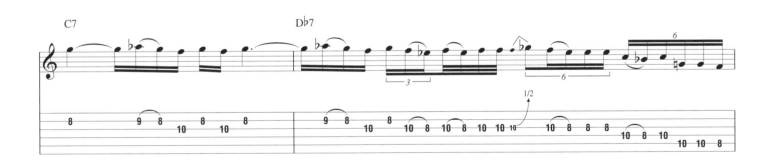

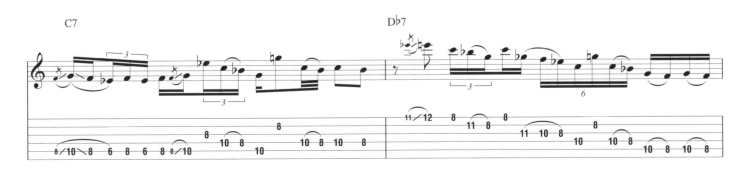

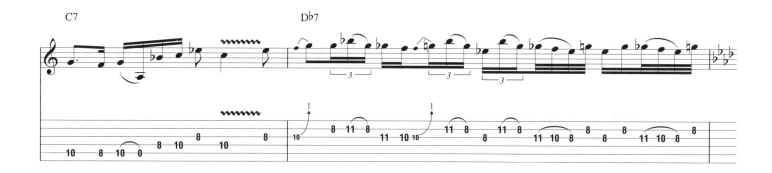

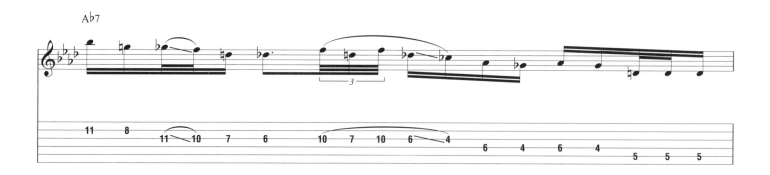

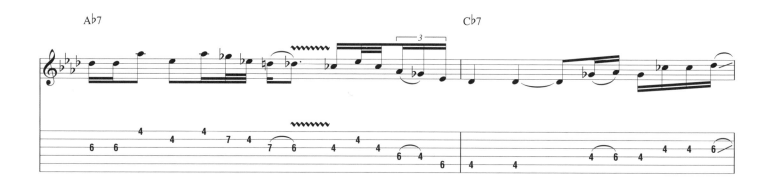

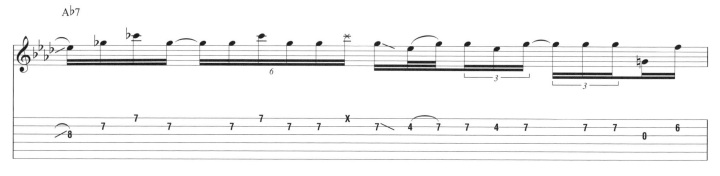

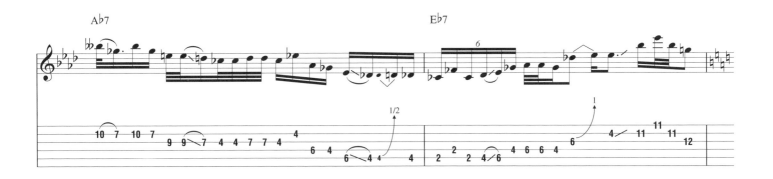

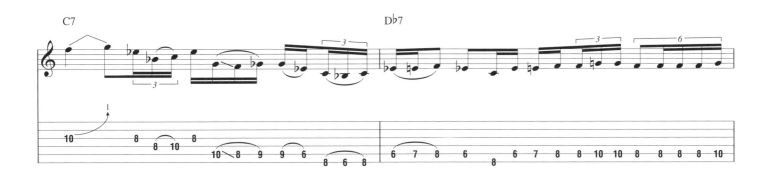

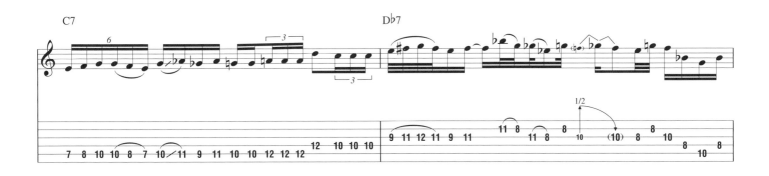

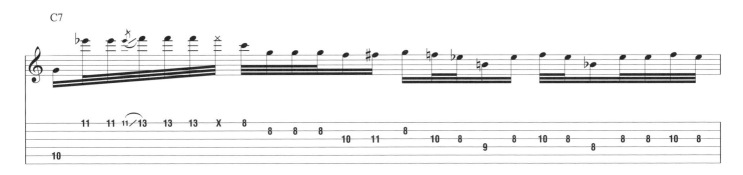

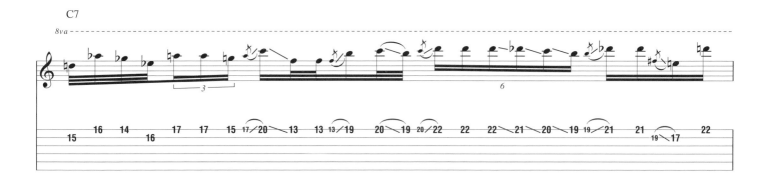

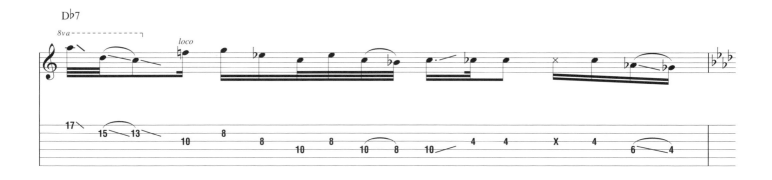

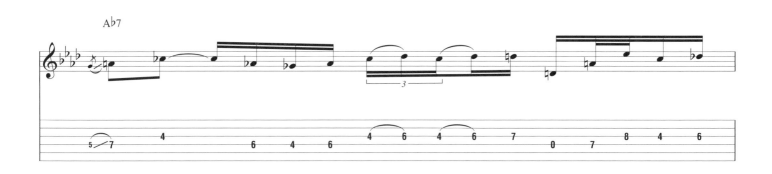

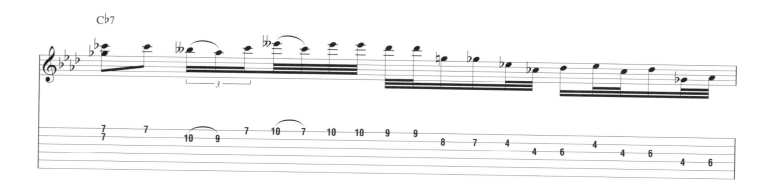

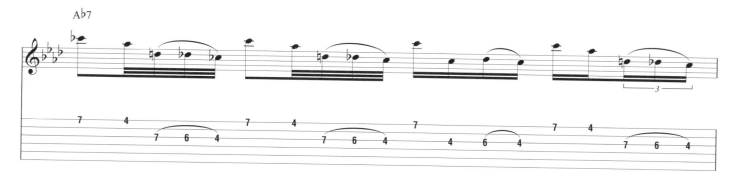

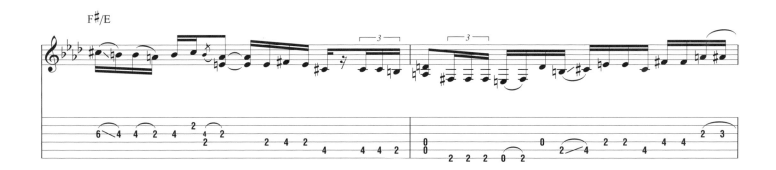

D.S. al Coda

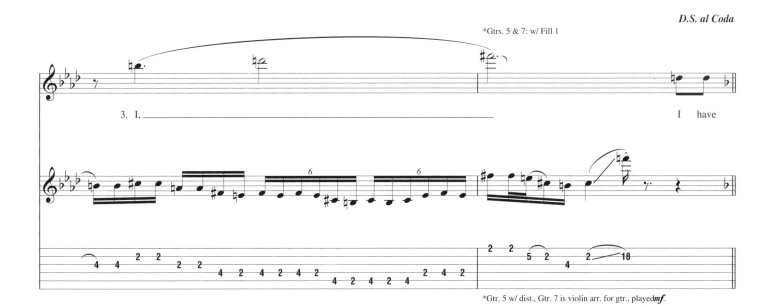

*Gtrs. 5 & 7: w/ Fill 1

3. I, _____ I have

Gtr. 5 w/ dist., Gtr. 7 is violin arr. for gtr., played **mf.*

⊕ Coda

Free time

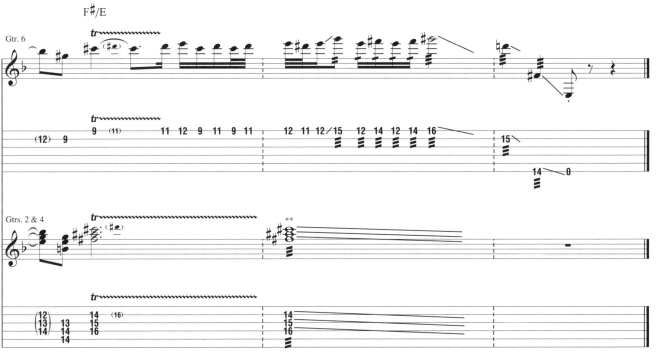

**Gtrs. 2 & 4 w/ random slides and trem. picking ad lib (till end).

Zomby Woof

By Frank Zappa

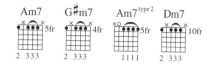

*Gtr. 1 is trumpet arr. for gtr., Gtr. 2 is vibes arr. for gtr., and Gtr. 4 is horns arr. for gtr.
**Chord symbols reflect overall harmony.

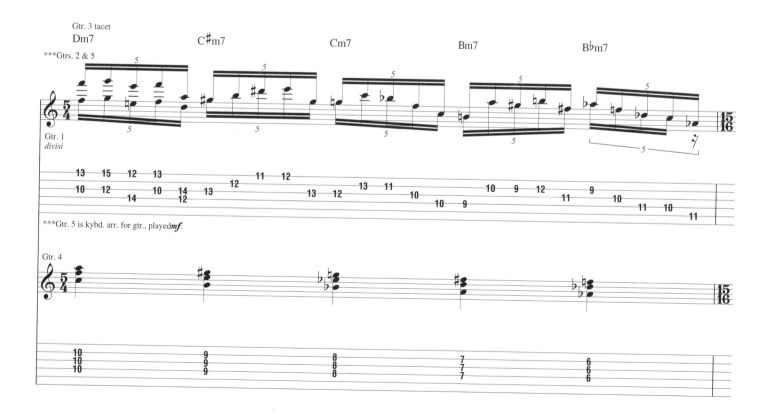

***Gtr. 5 is kybd. arr. for gtr., played *mf*.

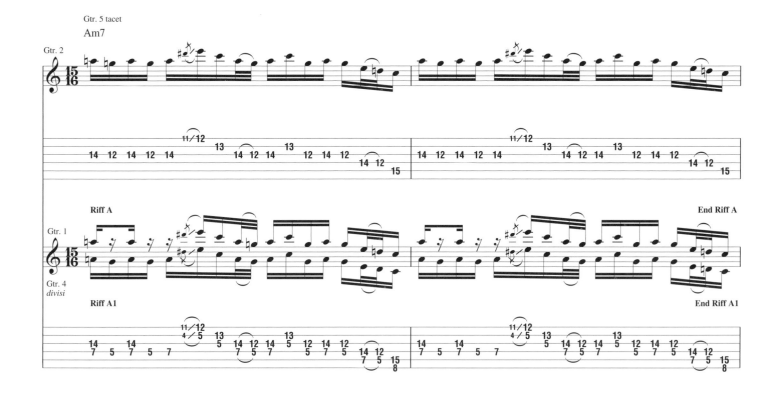

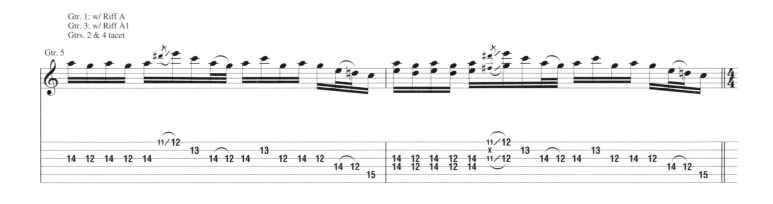

Verse

1. Three hun - dred years a - go ____ I thought I might get some sleep. ____ I

*Fuzz bass arr. for gtr.

stretched my-self out on-na an-tique bed,___ an' my spir-it did a mid-night creep.___

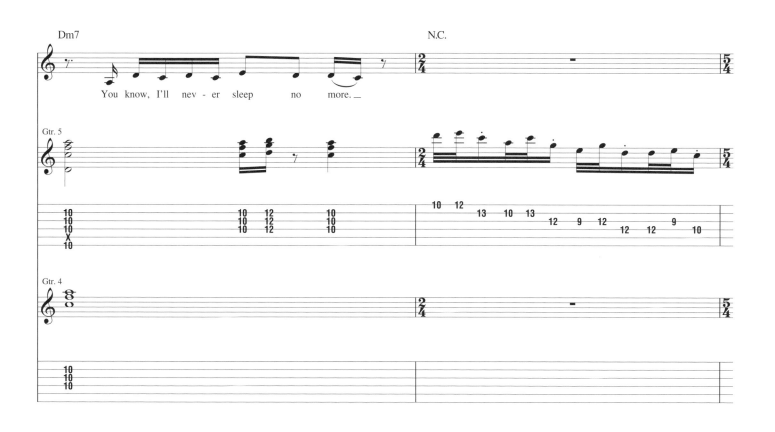

You know, I'll nev-er sleep no more.___

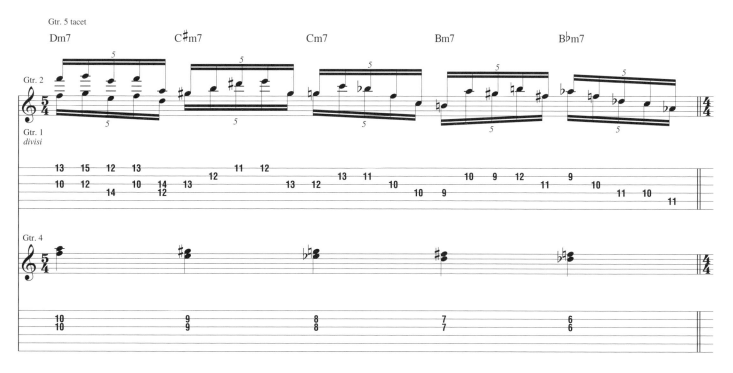

Verse

Gtrs. 1, 4 & 7 tacet

Am7

2. To me it seem __ that it just ain't wise.

Female: (Did - ja

P.M.

*Gtr. 7

Gtr. 5

Gtrs. 1 & 2
divisi

(Gtr. 2, cont. on lower staff)

*Pizz. violin arr. for gtr., played *mf*.

Gtr. 4

Gtr. 2

Gtr. 3
divisi

Gtr. 3
divisi

Bm7

Am7

ev - er wake __ up in the morn - in'...)

...with a Zom - by Woof __ be - hind your eyes? __

56

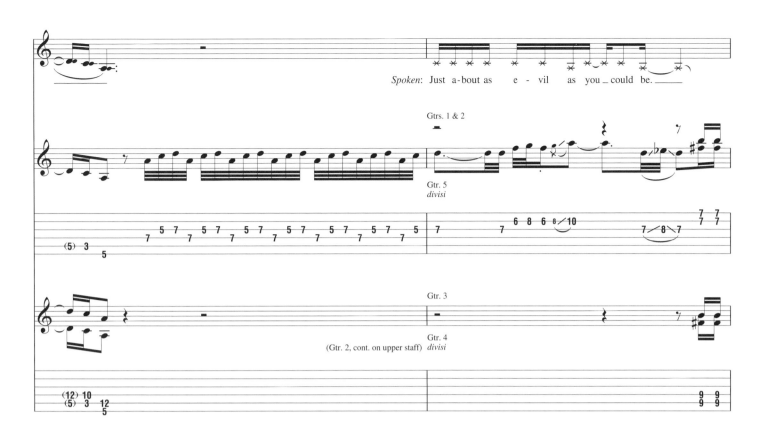

Spoken: Just a-bout as   e - vil   as   you_ could be. _____

Interlude

Slower ♩ = 76

Gtrs. 3 & 8 tacet

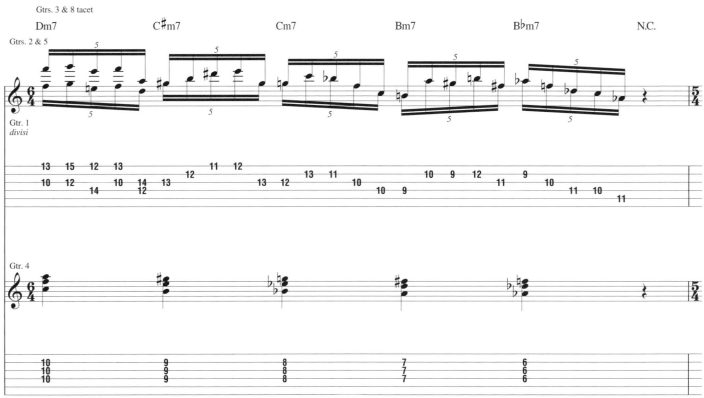

Gtr. 2 tacet

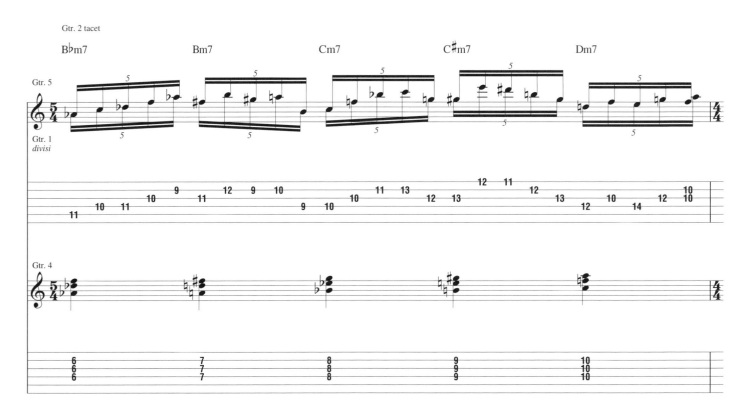

58

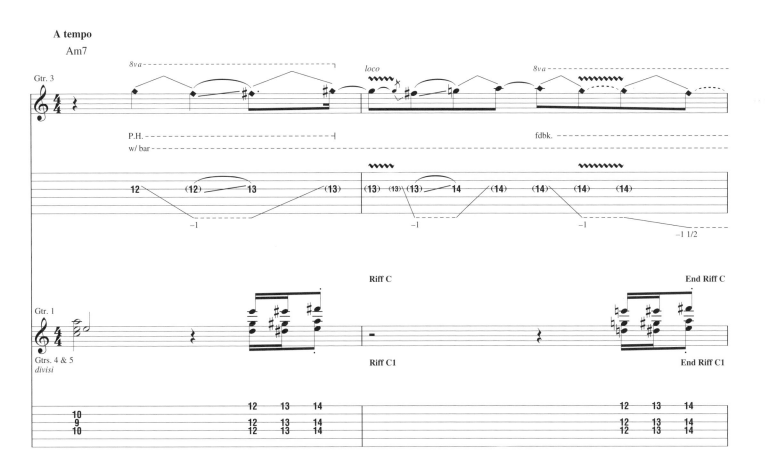

Gtrs. 1 & 4: w/ Riffs C & C1 (2 times)

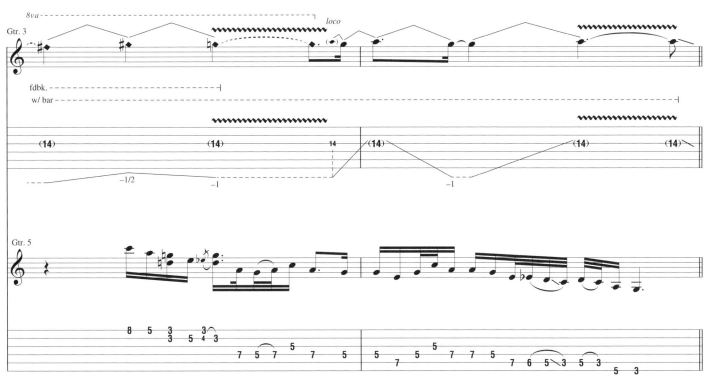

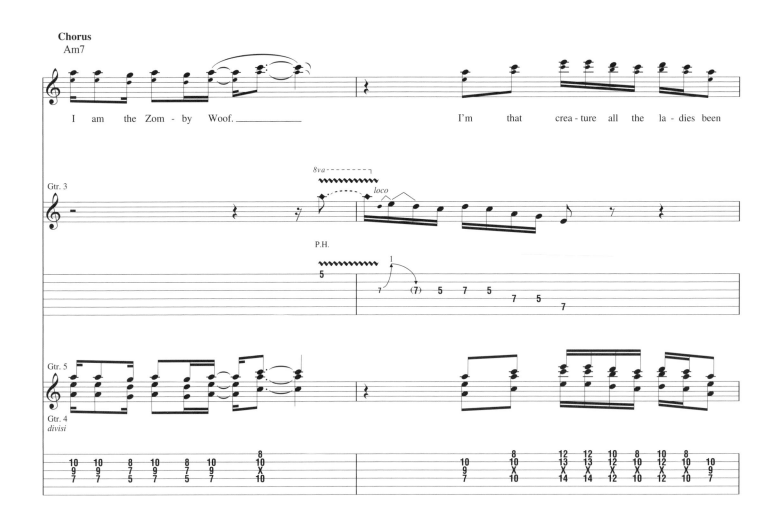

I am the Zom - by Woof. _____ I'm that crea - ture all the la - dies been

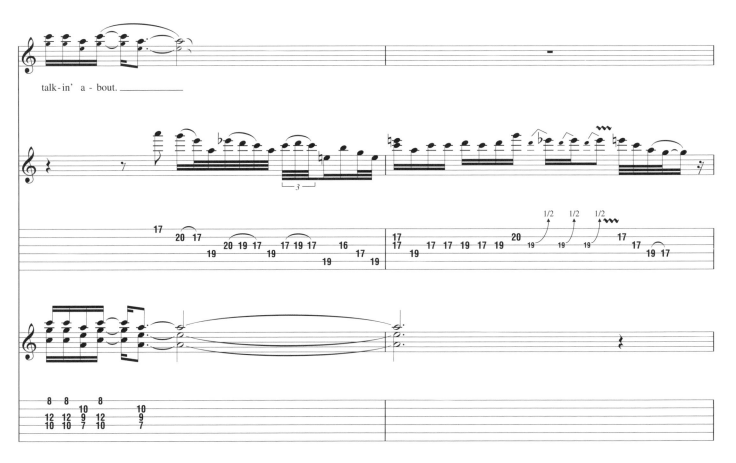

talk-in' a - bout. _____

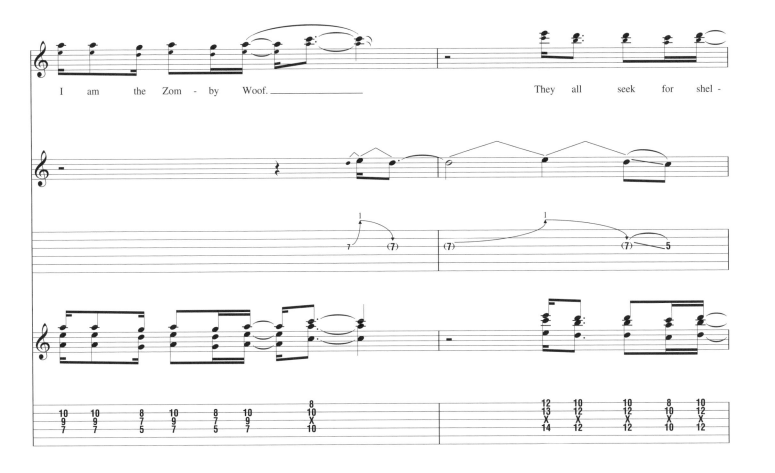

I am the Zom - by Woof._____ They all seek for shel -

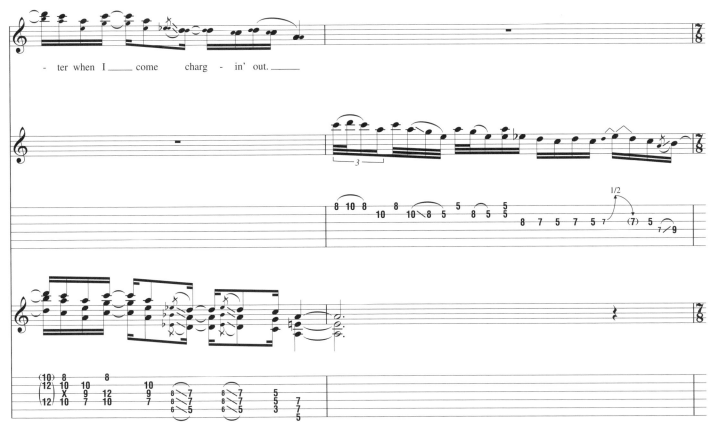

- ter when I ____ come charg - in' out. ____

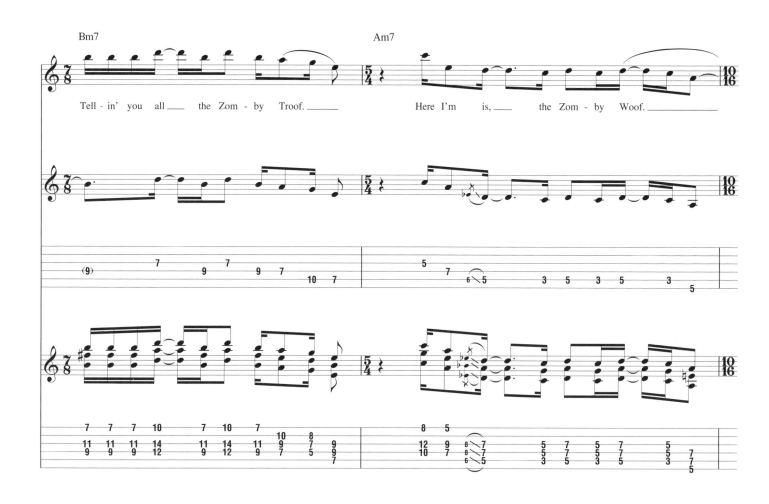

Tell - in' you all ___ the Zom - by Troof. ___ Here I'm is, ___ the Zom - by Woof. ___

Gtr. 9 tacet

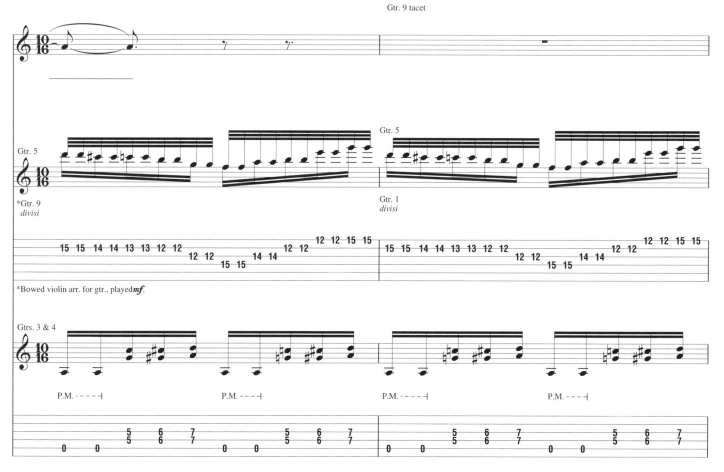

Gtr. 5

Gtr. 5

*Gtr. 9
divisi

Gtr. 1
divisi

*Bowed violin arr. for gtr., played *mf*.

Gtrs. 3 & 4

P.M. - - - -┘   P.M. - - - -┘   P.M. - - - -┘   P.M. - - - ┘

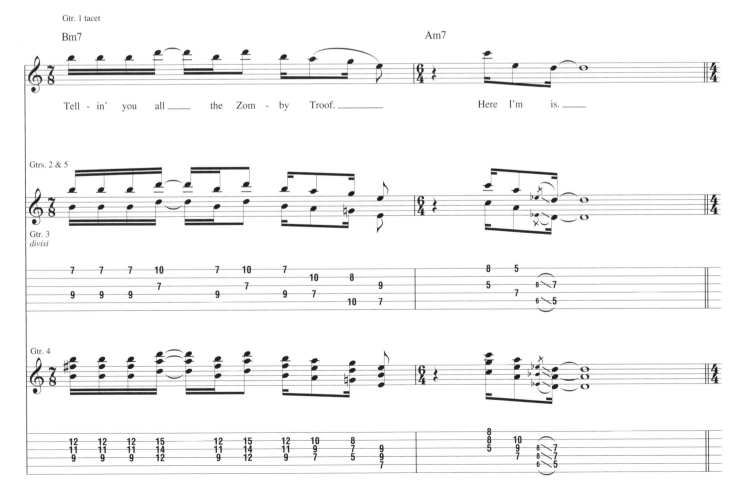

Interlude

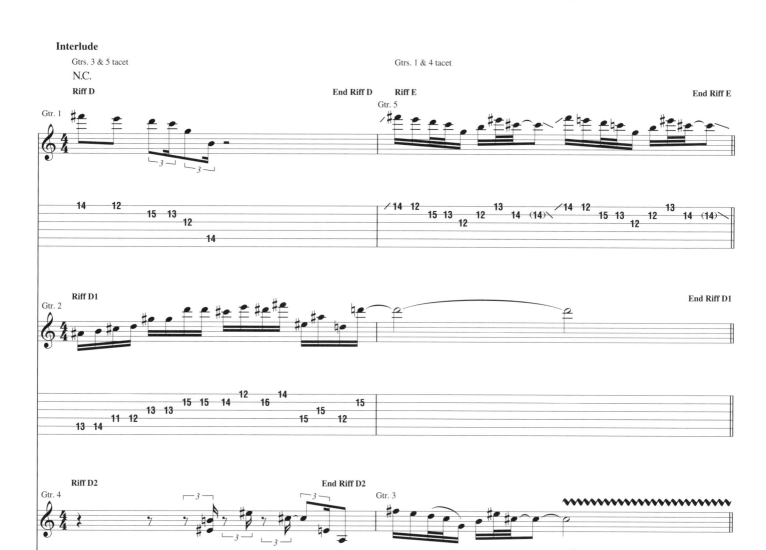

Bridge

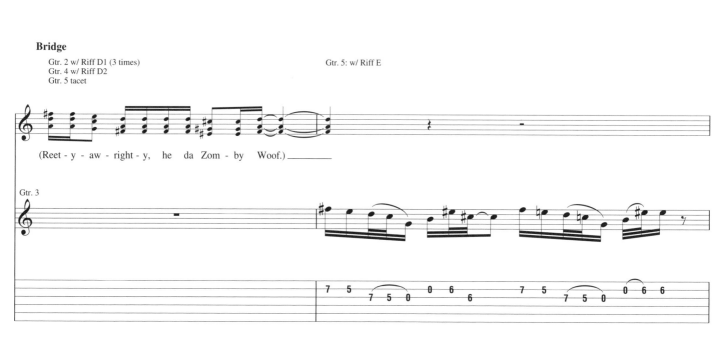

(Reet - y - aw - right - y, he da Zom - by Woof.)

Gtrs. 1 & 4: w/ Riffs D & D2

Gtr. 5: w/ Riff E

w/ bar

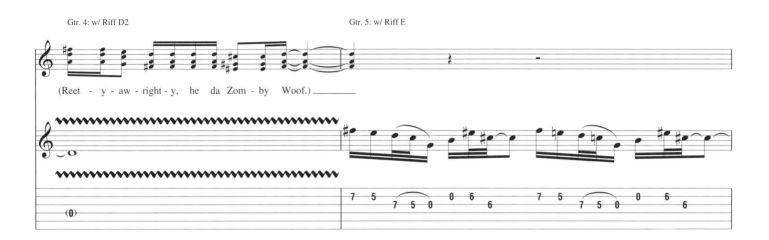

Gtr. 4: w/ Riff D2

Gtr. 5: w/ Riff E

(Reet - y - aw - right - y, he da Zom - by Woof.) _____

Am7

G#m7 Am7

G#m7 Am7

*Gtrs.
4 & 5

They said aw - reet - y, and they ___ was aw - right - y, an' I ___ was a Zom - by for you, lit - tle la - dy. ___

*Composite arrangement

Guitar Solo

Gtr. 4 tacet
Gtr. 5: ad lib comp. (next 36 meas.)

Am7

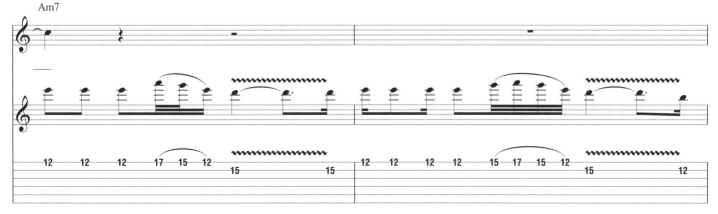

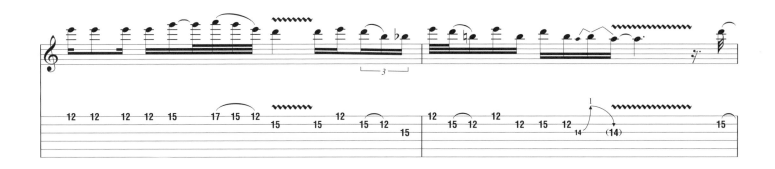

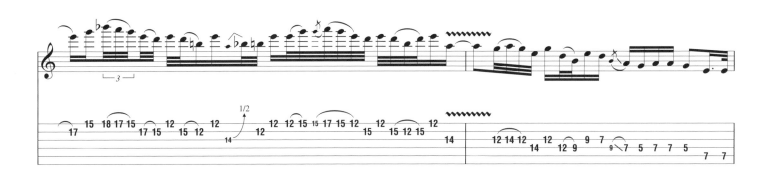

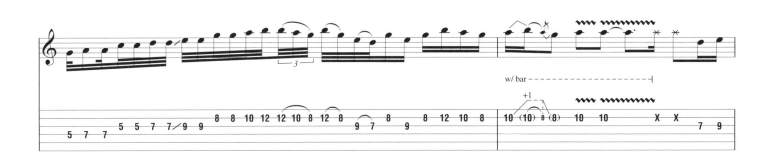

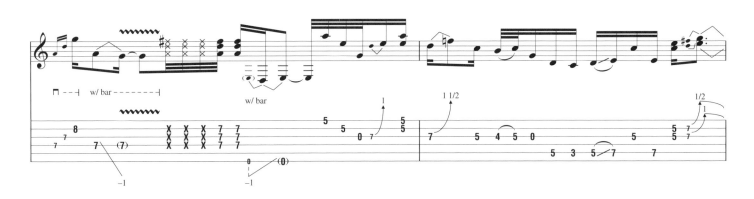

Pitch: G#

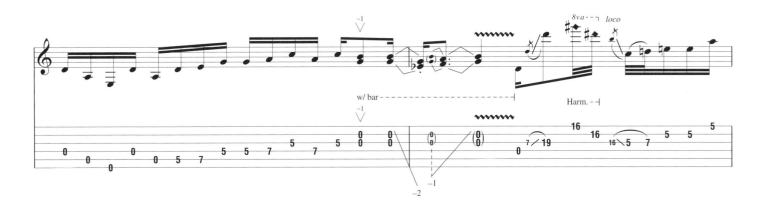

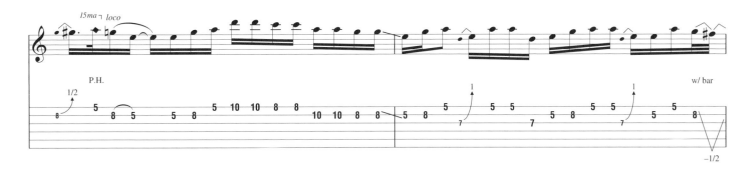

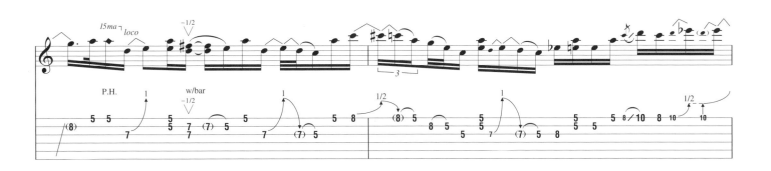

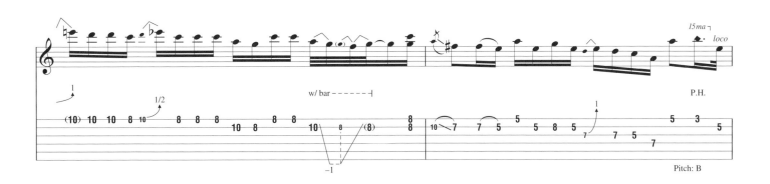

Pitch: B

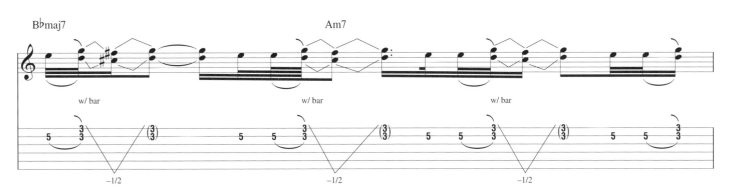

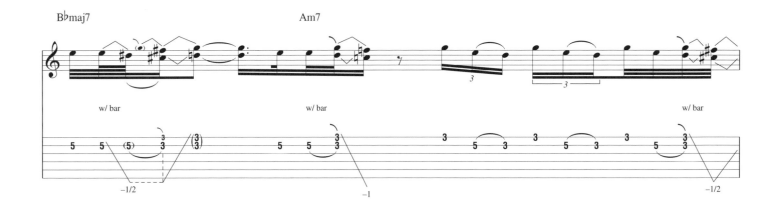

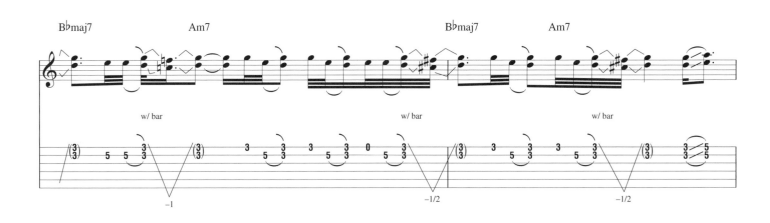

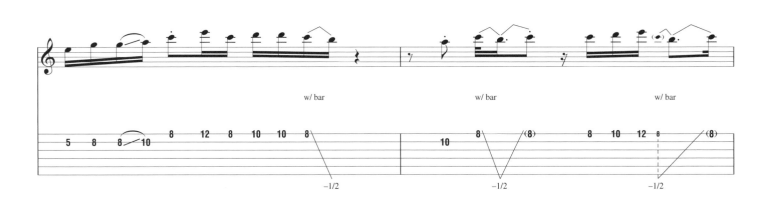

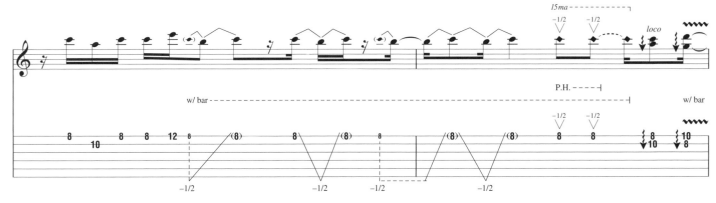

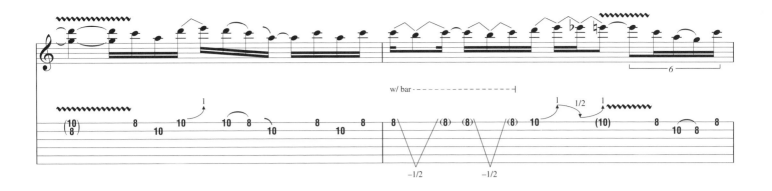

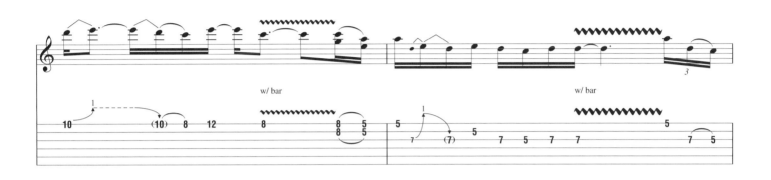

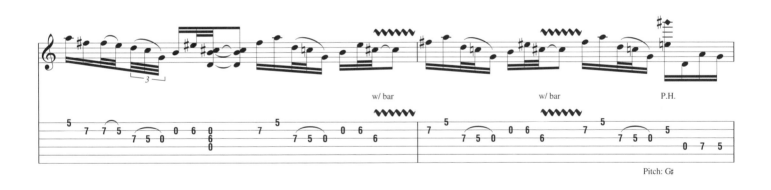

I got a

Bridge

great big point-ed fang, __ which is my Zom - by Toof. __ My

right foot's big-ger than my oth - er one is, __ like a reg - u - lar Zom - by Hoof. __ If I

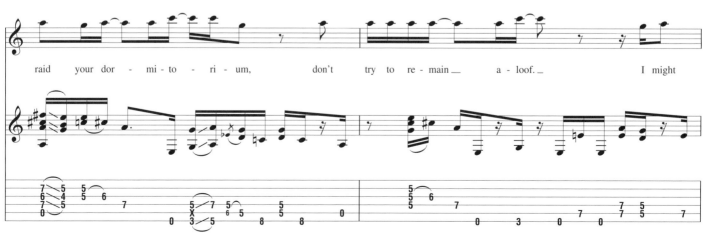

raid your dor - mi - to - ri - um, don't try to re - main __ a - loof. __ I might

snatch you up scream-in' through the win-dow all nek-kid, and do it to you up on the roof. Don't mess with the
(...and do it to you up on the roof. Don't mess with the

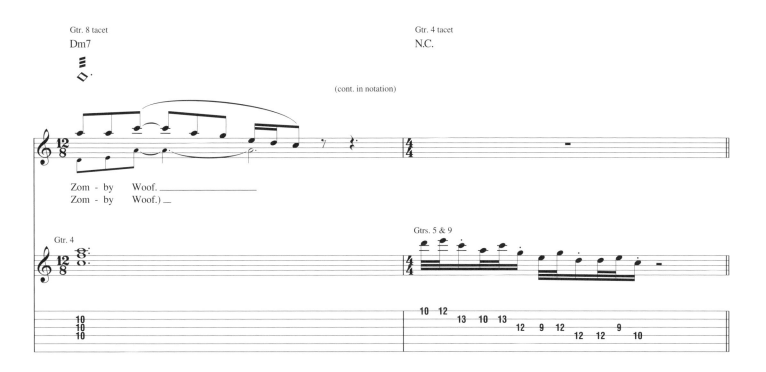

Zom - by Woof. _____
Zom - by Woof.) _

(cont. in notation)

Outro-Chorus

I am _____ a-bout as e - vil as a Boog-ie Man can be.

*Composite arrangement

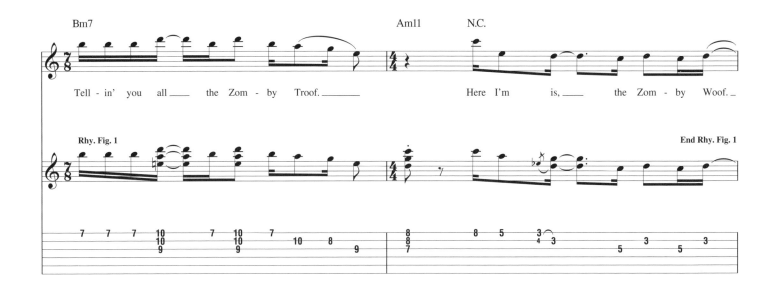

Tell - in' you all _____ the Zom - by Troof. _____   Here I'm is, _____ the Zom - by Woof. _

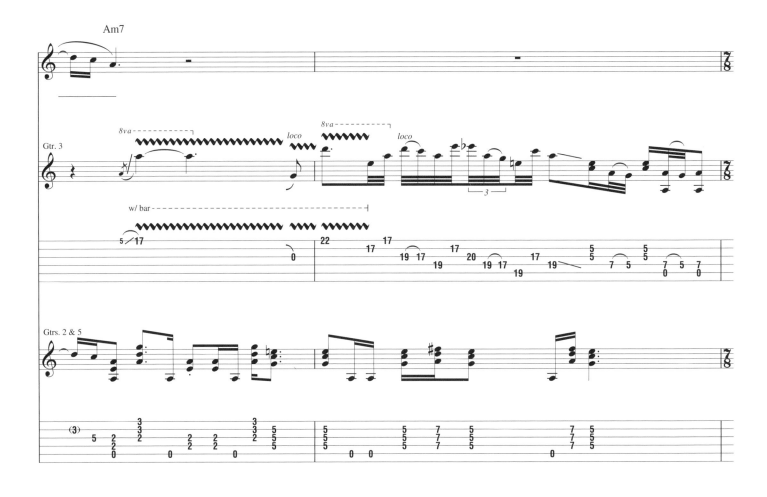

Gtrs. 2 & 5: w/ Rhy. Fig. 1 (simile)
Gtr. 3 tacet

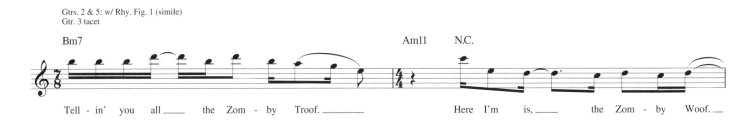

Tell - in' you all _____ the Zom - by Troof. _____   Here I'm is, _____ the Zom - by Woof. _

Dinah-Moe Humm

By Frank Zappa

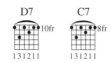

Intro
Moderately ♩ = 120

N.C.

Gtr. 1 (clean)

Rhy. Fig. 1

mf
w/ flanger

End Rhy. Fig. 1

1. I

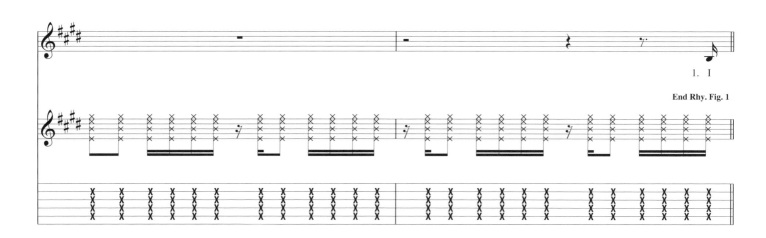

Verse

E   F#   E   D   A

could-n't say where she's com-in' from, __ but I just met a la-dy named Di-nah-Moe Humm.
bet with her sis-ter who's a lit-tle bit dumb, she could prove it an-y time all men was scum.
whipped off her bloom-ers 'n stiff-ened my thumb, an' ap-plied ro-ta-tion on her sug-ar plum.

Rhy. Fig. 2

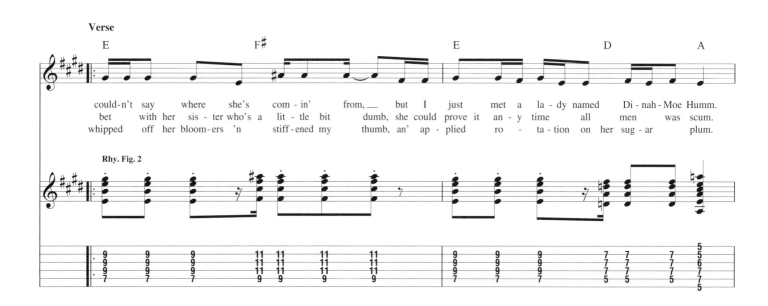

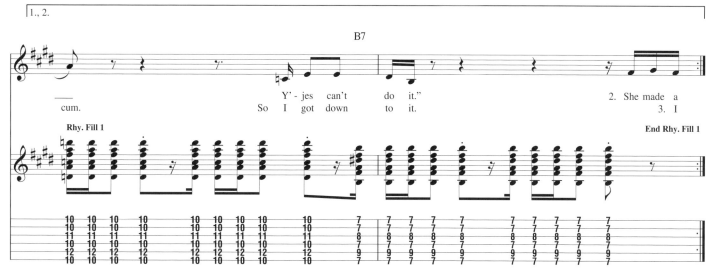

Di - nah - Moe _____ Humm. _

Chorus
Double-time feel

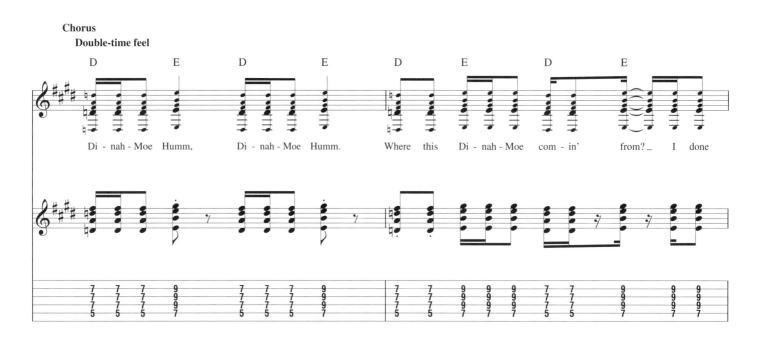

Di - nah - Moe Humm, Di - nah - Moe Humm. Where this Di - nah - Moe com - in' from? _ I done

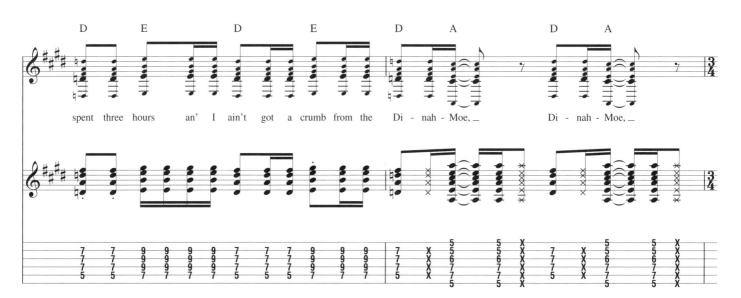

spent three hours an' I ain't got a crumb from the Di - nah - Moe, _ Di - nah - Moe, _

End double-time feel

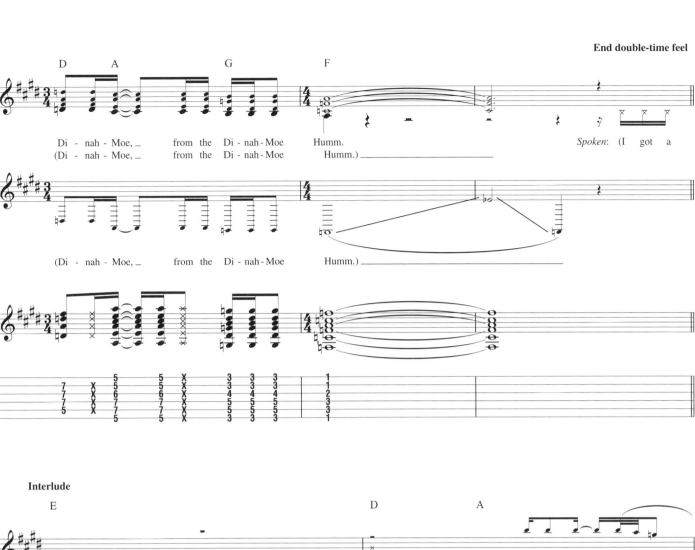

Interlude

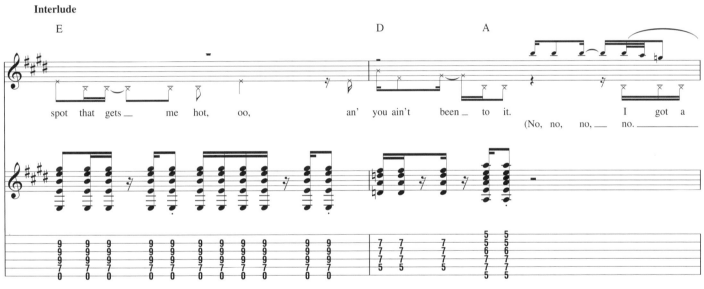

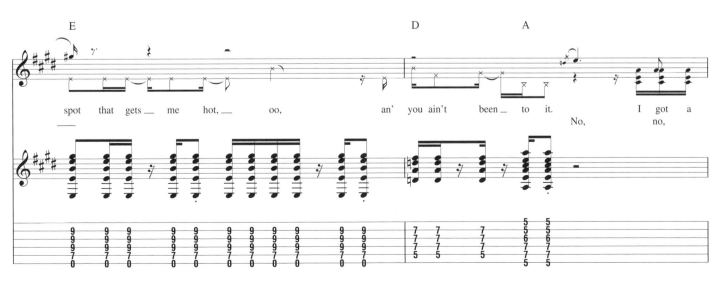

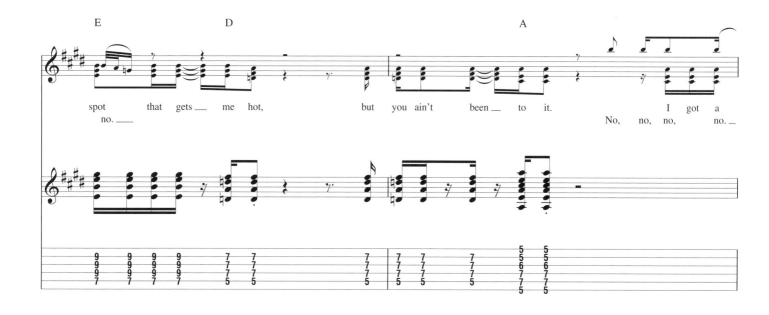

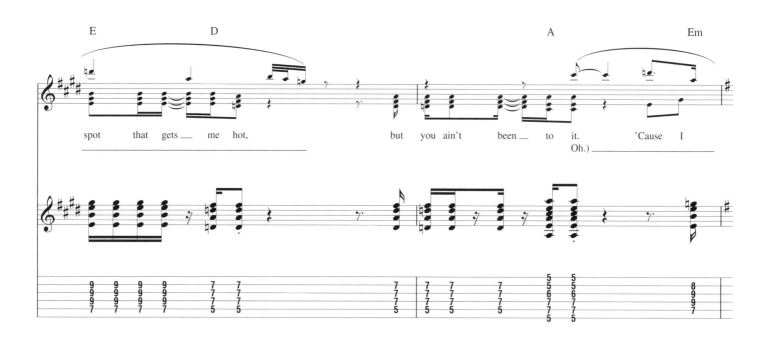

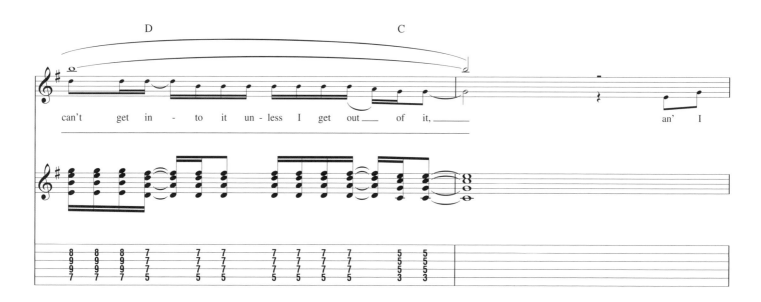

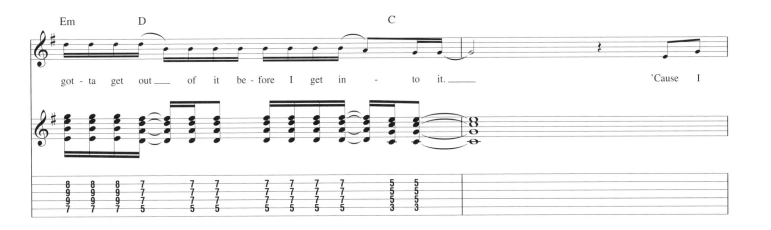

gotta get out of it before I get into it. 'Cause I

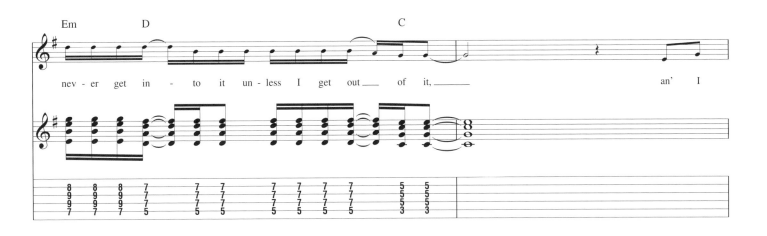

nev-er get in - to it un-less I get out of it, an' I

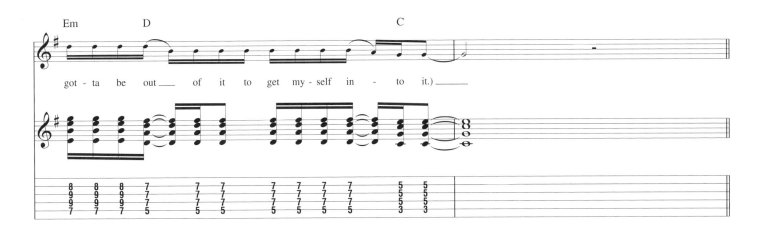

got - ta be out of it to get my - self in - to it.)

Bridge

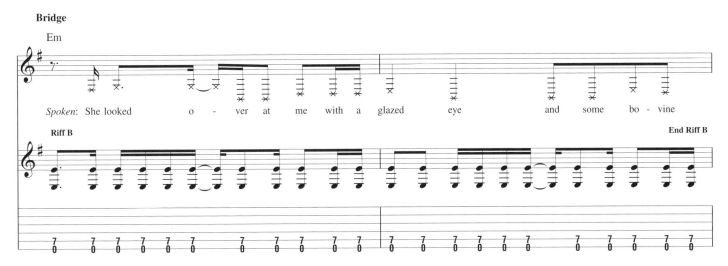

Spoken: She looked o - ver at me with a glazed eye and some bo - vine

Riff B

End Riff B

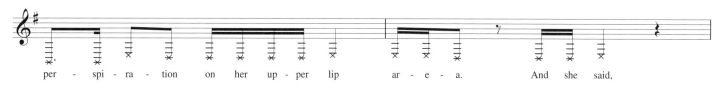

per - spi - ra - tion on her up - per lip ar - e - a. And she said,

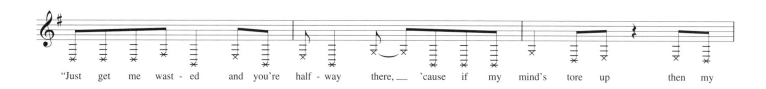

"Just get me wast - ed and you're half - way there, __ 'cause if my mind's tore up then my

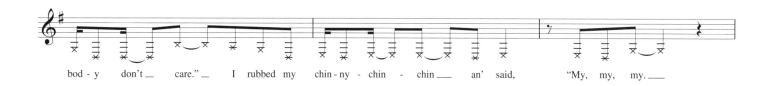

bod - y don't __ care." __ I rubbed my chin - ny - chin - chin __ an' said, "My, my, my. __

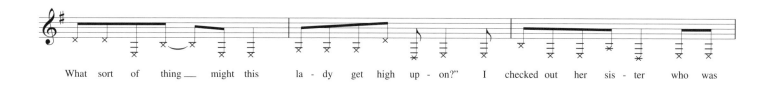

What sort of thing __ might this la - dy get high up - on?" I checked out her sis - ter who was

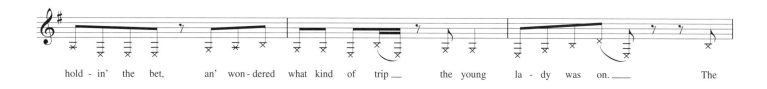

hold - in' the bet, an' won - dered what kind of trip __ the young la - dy was on. __ The

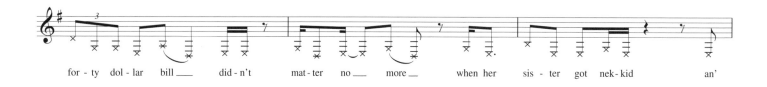

for - ty dol - lar bill __ did - n't mat - ter no __ more __ when her sis - ter got nek - kid an'

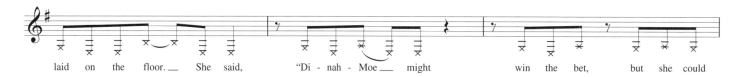

laid on the floor. __ She said, "Di - nah - Moe __ might win the bet, but she could

she start-ed in — to squeal-in'. — Di - nah - Moe watched from the

edge — of the bed with her lips just a - twitch - in' an' her face gone red. — Some

drool roll - in' down — from the edge of her chin — while she spied the con - di - tion her

sis - ter was in. — She quiv-ered 'n quaked — an' clutched at her - self while her

sis - ter made a joke a - bout her — men - tal health. — Till Di - nah - Moe — fi - nal - ly

— did give in, — but I told her all — she real - ly need-ed was some — dis - ci - pline. —

w/ kissing
Gtr. 1: w/ Rhy. Fig. 3 (12 times, simile)

Em11

Kiss my — au - ra, Do - ra.

(A - hoo.)

Rhy. Fig. 3   End Rhy. Fig. 3
Gtr. 1

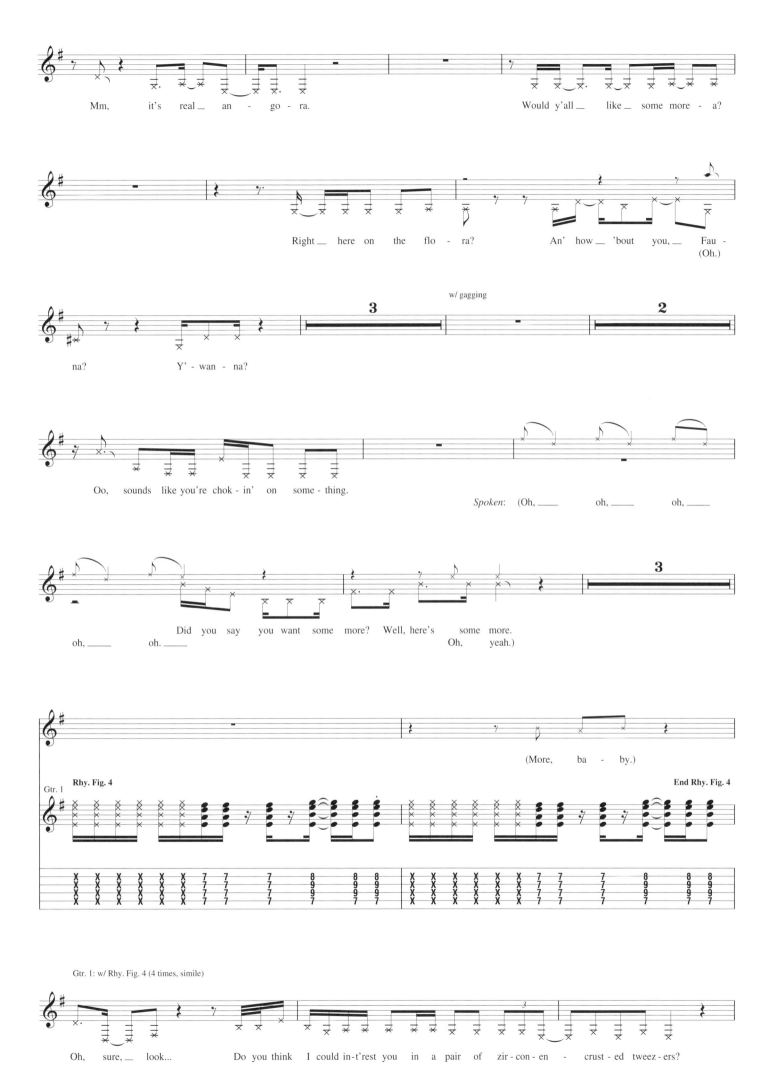

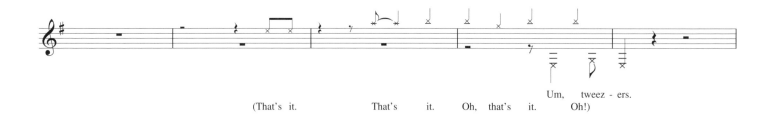

(That's it. That's it. Oh, that's it. Oh!) Um, tweez-ers.

Gtr. 1

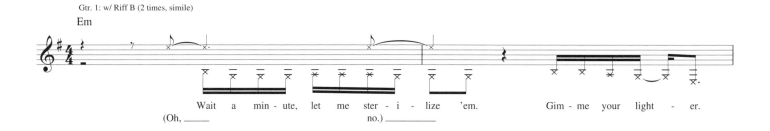

Gtr. 1: w/ Riff B (2 times, simile)

Em

Wait a min-ute, let me ster-i-lize 'em. Gim-me your light-er.
(Oh, ___ no.) ___

Gtr. 1: w/ Rhy. Fig. 1

2   3

4. I

Verse

Gtr. 1: w/ Rhy. Fig. 2

E   F#   E   D   A

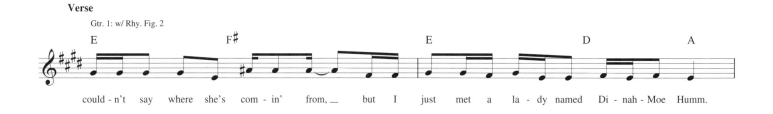

could-n't say where she's com-in' from, ___ but I just met a la-dy named Di-nah-Moe Humm.

Gtr. 2: w/ Riff A

Am11 G#m11#5 Gm13 F#m7   E   F#

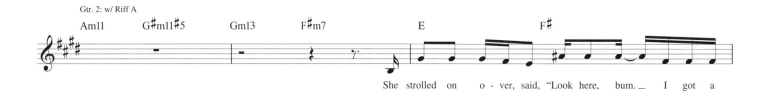

She strolled on o-ver, said, "Look here, bum. ___ I got a

Gtr. 1: w/ Rhy. Fill 1

G   G7   D7   B7

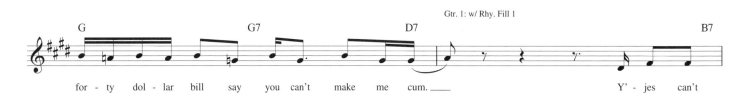

for-ty dol-lar bill say you can't make me cum. ___ Y'- jes can't

Verse

Gtr. 1: w/ Rhy. Fig. 2

do it.   5. I whipped off her bloom-ers 'n stiff-ened my thumb, an' ap-

Gtr. 2: w/ Riff A

plied ro-ta-tion on her sug-ar plum.   I

poked 'n stroked till my wrist got numb, an' you know I heard___ some Di-nah-Moe_____ Humm,___

Outro

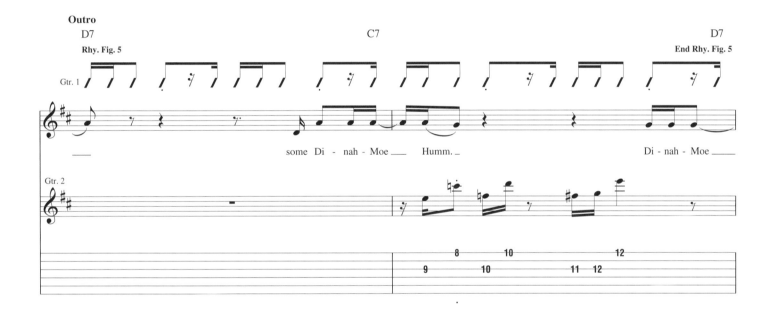

Play 9 times and fade

2nd time, w/ Ld. Voc. ad lib (till fade)
Gtr. 1: w/ Rhy. Fig. 5 (till fade)

Montana

By Frank Zappa

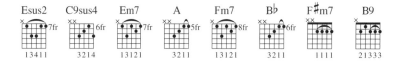

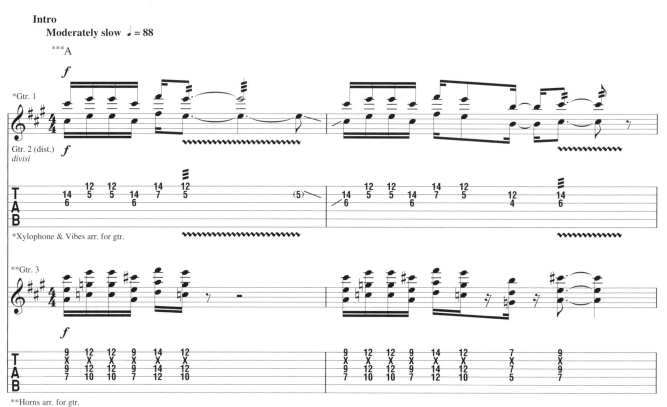

*Xylophone & Vibes arr. for gtr.

**Horns arr. for gtr.

***Chord symbols reflect overall harmony.

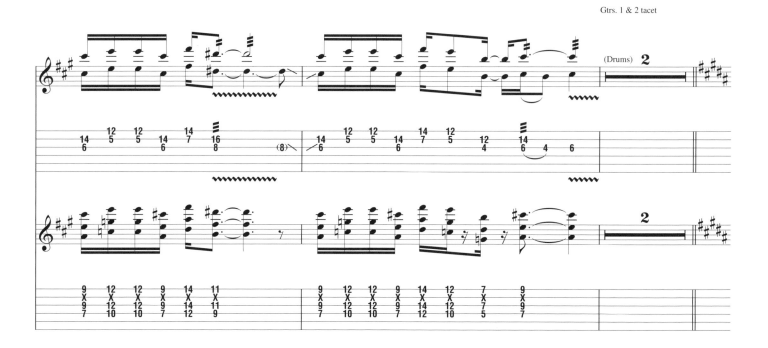

Verse

Spoken: 1. I might be mov-in' to Mon-tan-a soon, just to raise me up a crop of

den-tal floss. _ Rais-in' it up, wax-en it down

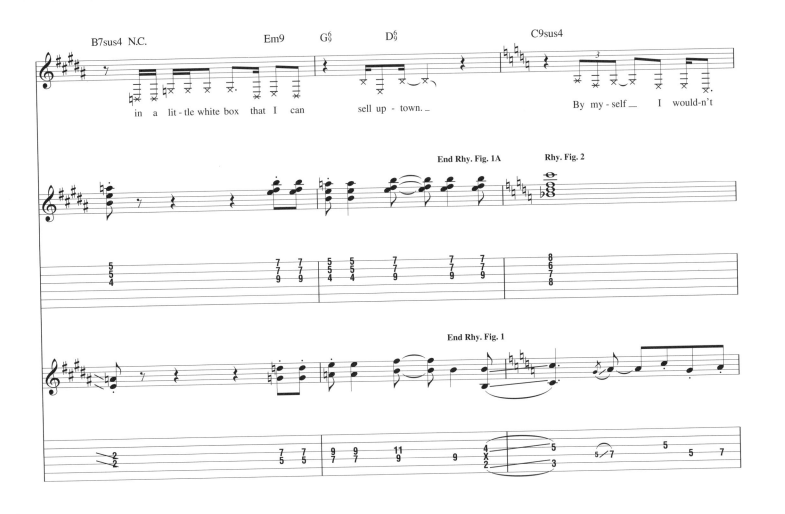

in a lit-tle white box that I can sell up-town. By my-self I would-n't

End Rhy. Fig. 1A   Rhy. Fig. 2

End Rhy. Fig. 1

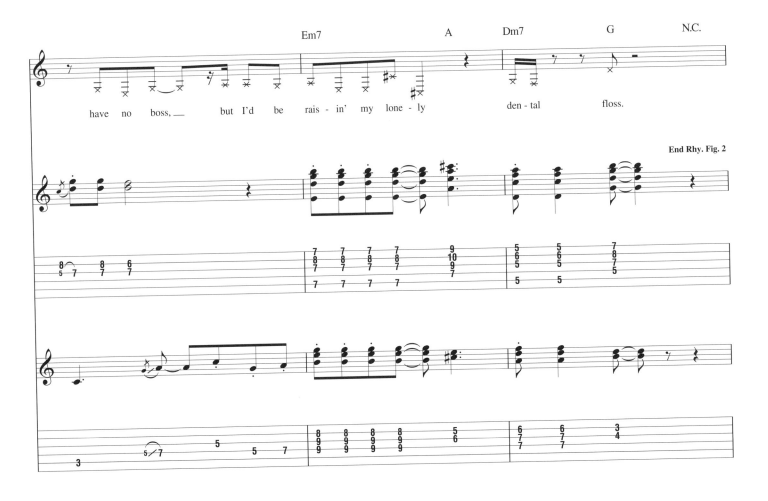

have no boss, but I'd be rais-in' my lone-ly den-tal floss.

End Rhy. Fig. 2

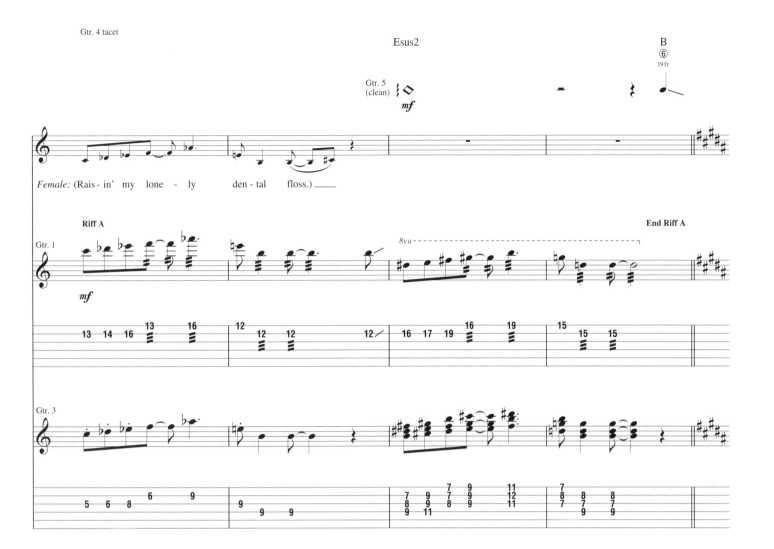

Verse

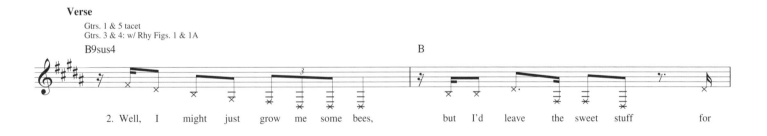

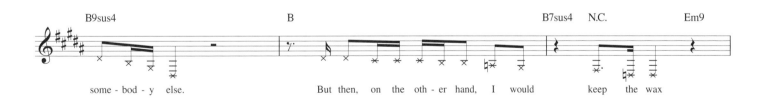

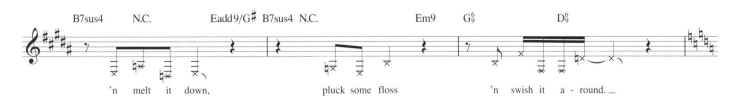

C9sus4

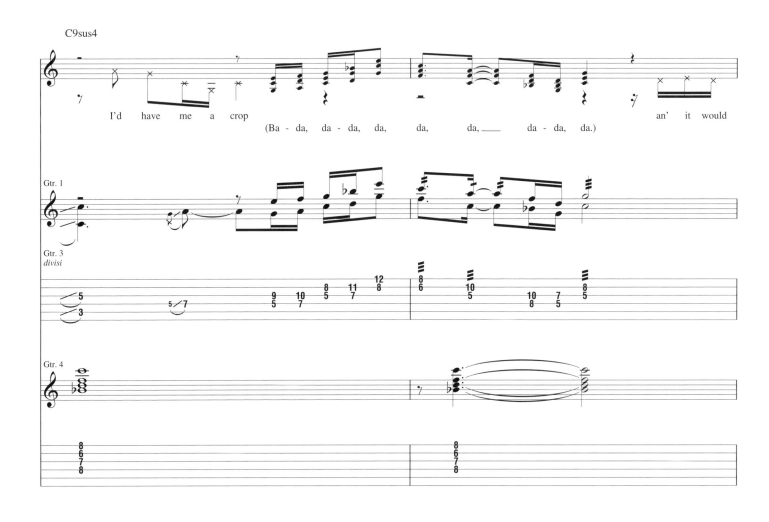

I'd have me a crop
(Ba - da, da - da, da,   da,   da, ____ da - da, da.)
an' it would

Gtr. 1

Gtr. 3
divisi

Gtr. 4

Gtr. 3 tacet

Em7   A   Fm7   B♭

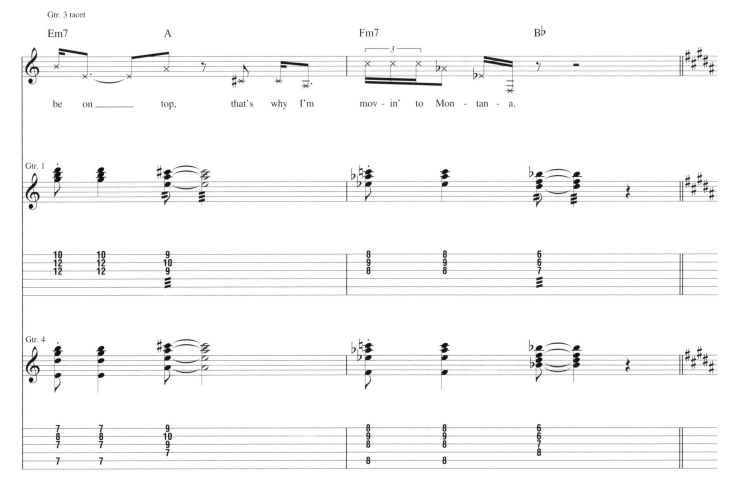

be on ____ top,   that's why I'm   mov - in' to Mon - tan - a.

Gtr. 1

Gtr. 4

Gtr. 1 tacet

B9sus4

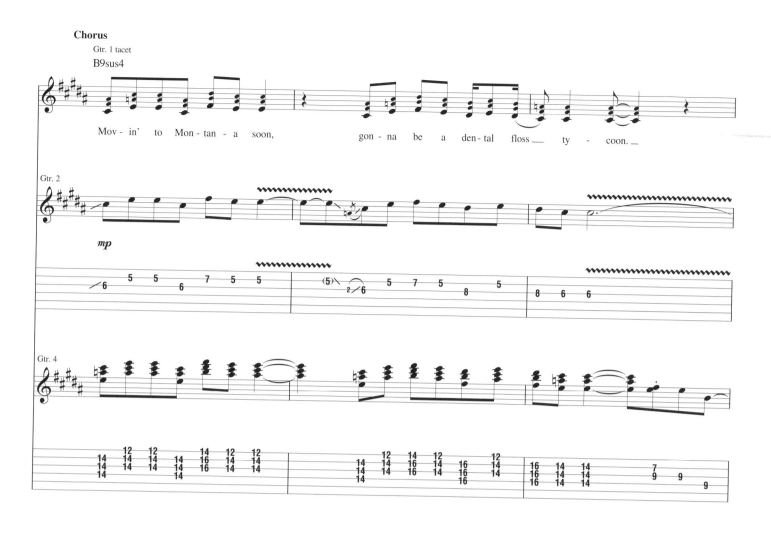

Mov - in' to Mon - tan - a soon, gon - na be a den - tal floss ___ ty - coon. ___

Spoken: Yes, I am.

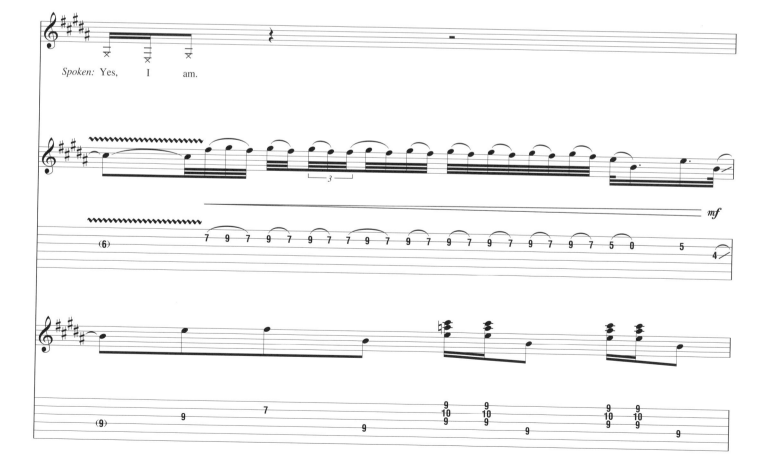

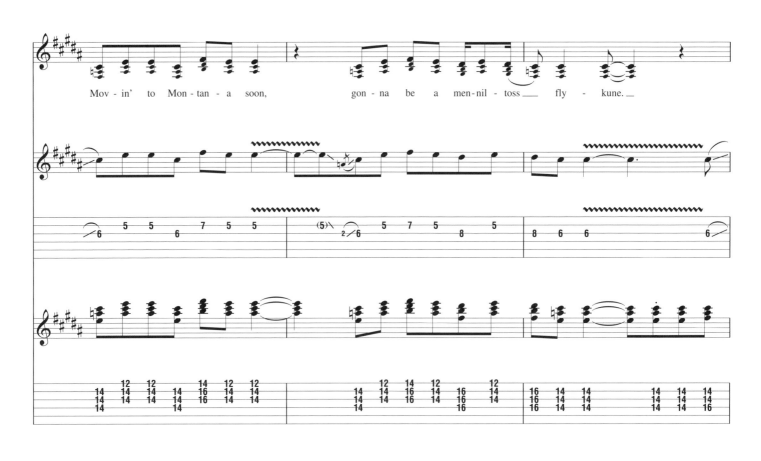

Mov - in' to Mon - tan - a soon, gon - na be a men - nil - toss___ fly - kune.___

Guitar Solo

Gtr. 4: w/ ad lib comp. (next 32 meas.)

F#m7

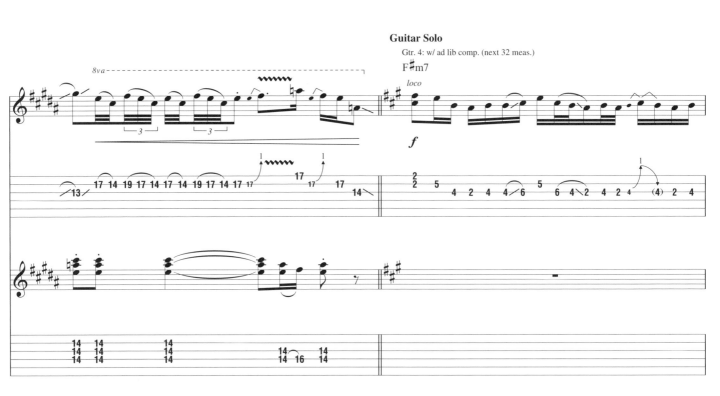

Gtr. 2

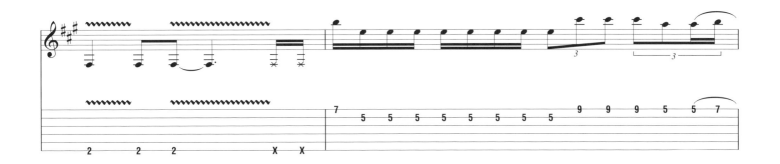

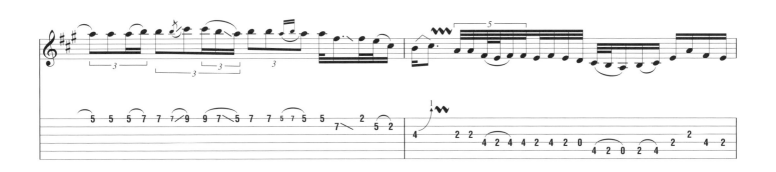

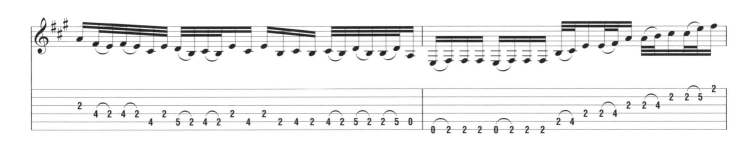

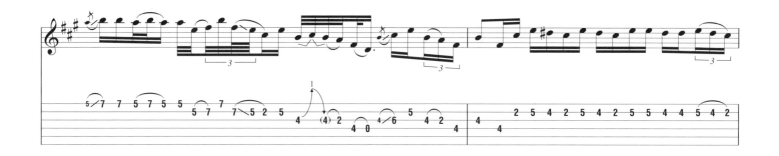
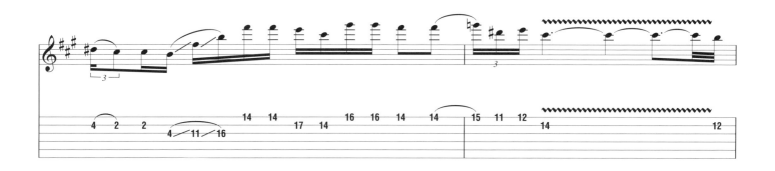
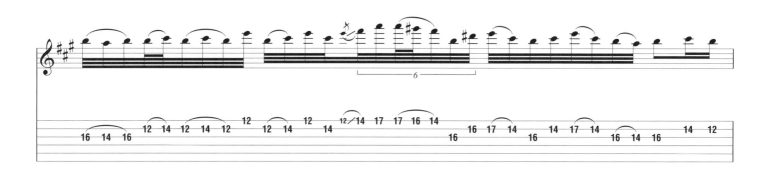
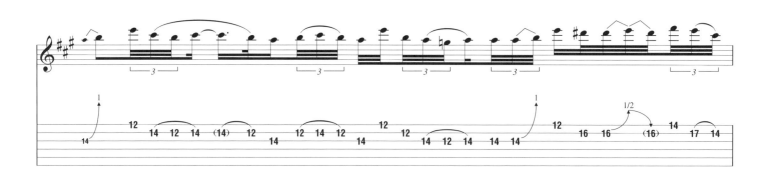
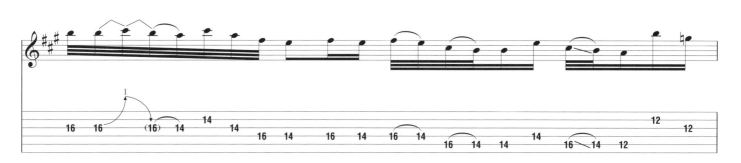

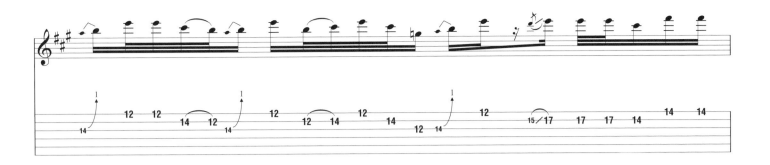

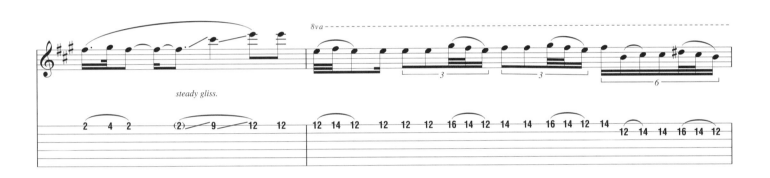

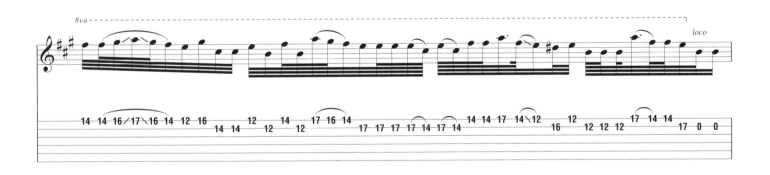

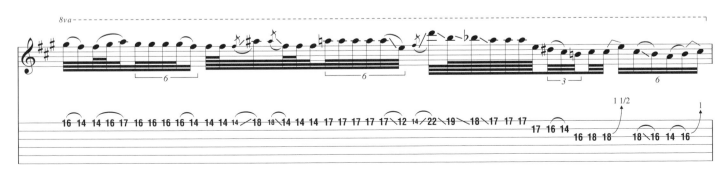

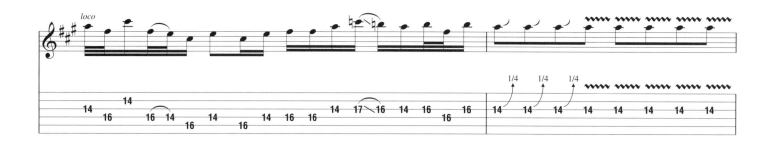

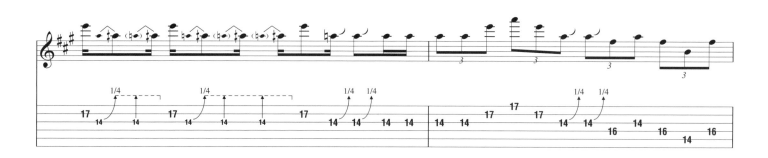

Bridge

Gtr. 2 tacet

N.C.

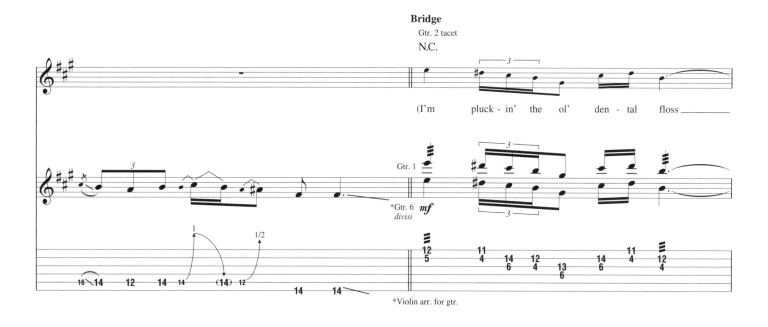

(I'm pluck - in' the ol' den - tal floss _____

*Violin arr. for gtr.

_____ that's grow - in' on the prai - rie. Pluck - in' the floss! I plucked all

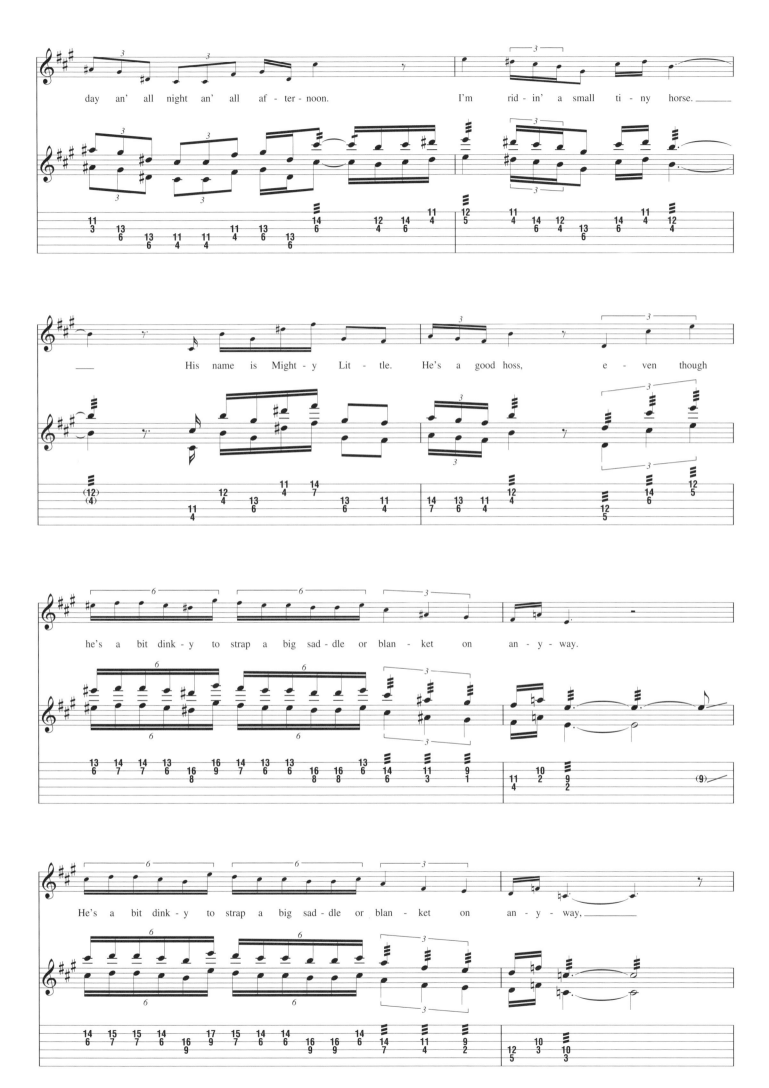

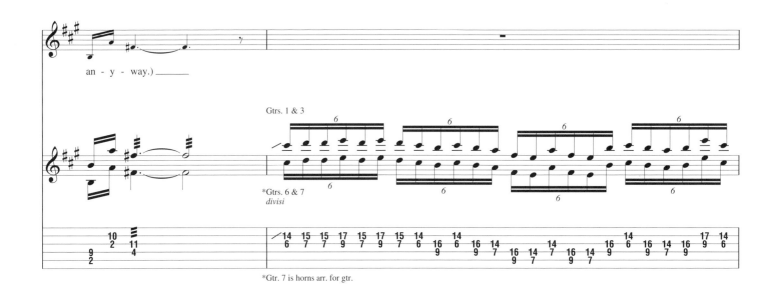

an - y - way.) _____

*Gtr. 7 is horns arr. for gtr.

(I'm pluck-in' the ol' den - tal floss, e - ven if you think it is a lit - tle sil - ly, folks.

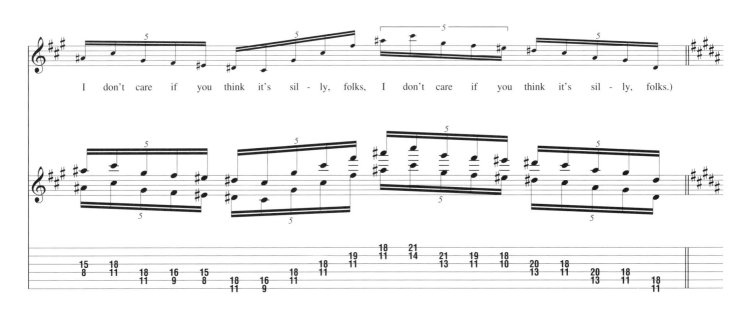

I don't care if you think it's sil - ly, folks, I don't care if you think it's sil - ly, folks.)

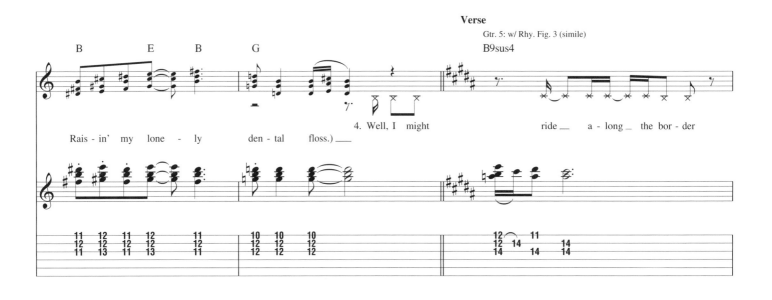

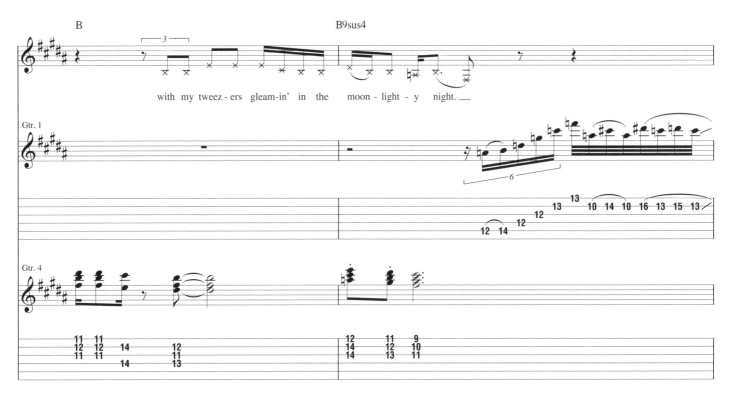

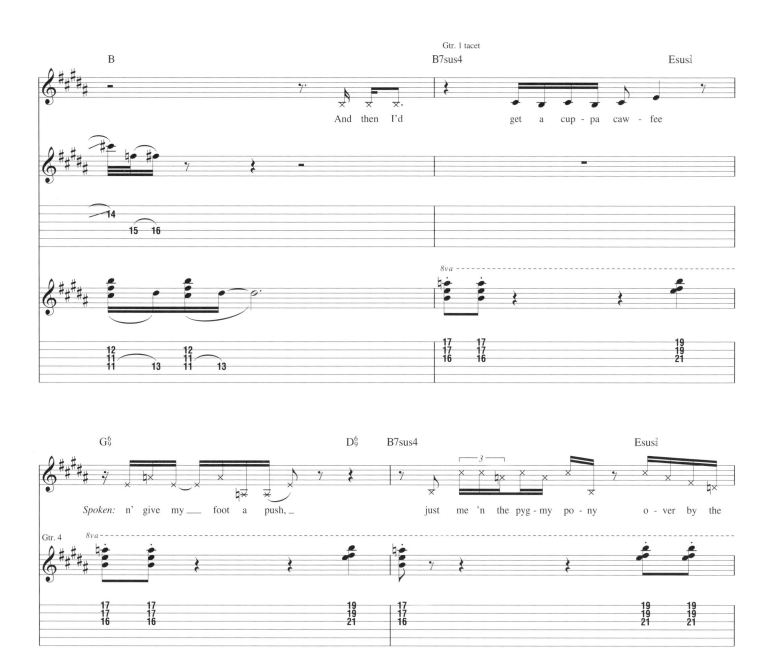

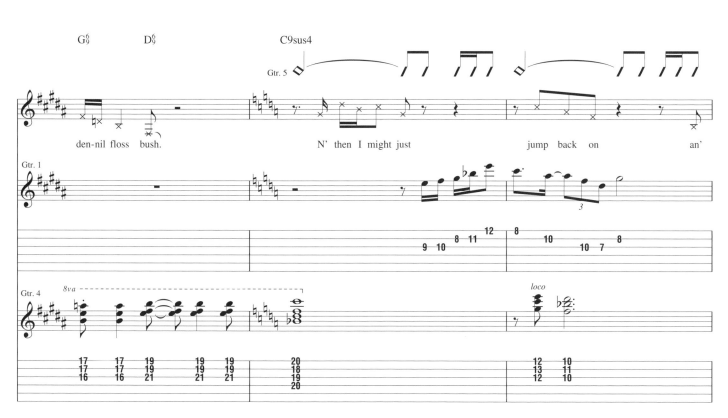

ride   like a cow - boy   in - to   the   dawn _____ to Mon - tan - a.

Outro

Gtr. 1 tacet

Gtr. 5

(Mov - in'   to   Mon - tan - a   soon.   Yip - py - ty   o - ty - ay. _____

Gtr. 4

Play 6 times and fade

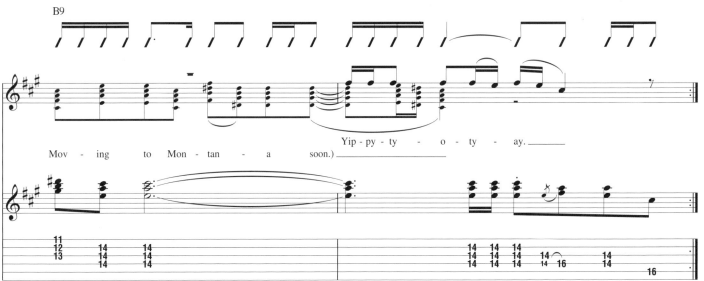

Mov - ing   to   Mon - tan - a   soon.) _____   Yip - py - ty   o - ty - ay. _____